Praises for

Ouch! When Ministry Hurts

A large portion of my current assignment in the Body of Christ is to help wounded servants. Will Sanborn's book, "Ouch! When Ministry Hurts," is a tremendous tool to help Christian workers gain perspective and perseverance in their specific ministry assignments. Every Christ-one who is serving in any capacity needs to read this book. Highly recommended!"

—Scott Mathis, President of the Berean Fellowship of Churches

***

Serving in ministry often comes with misconceptions from those in the community you serve. Who would not love to get paid to hang out with kids or adults, take them to do fun things, and talk to them about their faith? But the reality is, ministry is often difficult and quite lonely. In his book, "Ouch! When Ministry Hurts," Will Sanborn talks about the elements of ministry that often get neglected. He provides amazing insight from his own experiences, while encouraging those serving in any sort of ministry capacity. I wish I'd had this book as I was starting my journey, but I love that I have it as an encouragement now as I continue pursuing ministry.

—**Hope Mango,** Club Beyond Community Director (Young Life Military), Fort Hood, Texas

***

This is a must-read for anyone in ministry, whether professional or lay. The insights that Will Sanborn presents from everyday experiences are practical and applicable to today's culture.

Authentic! Encouraging! Hope-filled! If you work with people, you will be touched by the principles and advice you will glean.

—**Rev. Mark Brunott,** Pastor of Congregational Care, First Evangelical Free Church, Lincoln, Nebraska

***

The most balanced approach to ministry ever written! This book provides a tough reality of answering the call. Although the pain does not compare to what Christ experienced on the cross, the day-to-day struggles of working with paid or volunteer workers, to working with church board members, can leave lasting scars in support of Christian ministry. This book will make you take a hard look at ministry expounding on the plentiful blessings as well as the plentiful pain of the call.

—**Pinkie Fischer, Chaplain,** Lieutenant Colonel, U.S. Army Chaplain Corps

***

Ministry mirrors life. Times of joy are offset by tears of sorrow. Yet the grace of God enables the faithful servant of Christ to continue to press on. "Ouch!" reminds us to keep looking toward the finish line, not for an off-ramp. Read, be encouraged, and most importantly, keep pressing on.

—J. Paul Nyquist, Ph.D., Vice President of
Discipleship College of Biblical Studies, Houston, Texas

***

Despite all the difficulties and failures, I have experienced in ministry work, starting as a youth pastor, and continuing as an Army chaplain, I believe the core reason I was able to continue in ministry was because of the love and godly leadership of a man I met in the fall of 1987. That man was Will Sanborn. Before I even met him, a friend told me, "Will is solid, Will is faithful, you'll never regret working with him and for him." He was right.

I always felt Will believed in me. He gave me perspective and helped me learn to laugh at myself. Patient and speaking the truth in love, he shepherded me through many of life's trials. I am so grateful for the Lord bringing Will into my life. As you read this book, you'll see what I mean: Best teammate ever!

—Rev. Paul Foreman, Chaplain, Major, U.S. Army
Chaplain Corps (Ret.)

OUCH!

When Ministry Hurts

By Will Sanborn

Published by KHARIS PUBLISHING, imprint of KHARIS
MEDIA LLC.

ISBN-13: 978-1-63746-137-2
ISBN-10: 1-63746-137-2

Library of Congress Control Number: 2022939198

All KHARIS PUBLISHING products are available at special
quantity discounts for bulk purchase for sales promotions,
premiums, fund-raising, and educational needs. For details,
contact:

Kharis Media LLC
Tel: 1-479-599-8657
support@kharispublishing.com
www.kharispublishing.com

FOREWORD

Will Sanborn captures the challenges of ministry beautifully in "Ouch!" There is no doubt that ministry can be one of the most rewarding professions one could ever experience. At the same time, it can be exceedingly difficult for both the Christian worker and for his or her family.

Will methodically walks us through his rich journey of fifty years of ministry. He paints a beautiful picture of both the joys and dangers of ministry. This is a must read for all those who are in ministry leadership or who are preparing to launch into ministry of any kind.

You will be challenged by this book and you will not be disappointed. With more than thirty years in ministry myself, including coaching chaplains and pastors around the world, I found "Ouch" to be helpful in understanding the narrative of being a leader and minister in the Lord's church. Will also encourages the reader to serve God and never quit, doing what He has called us to do -- to "Soldier On."

No matter what your background, organization or denomination, this book provides the essential ingredients of ministry, of leading God's people, and how to navigate and deal with the reality that is called "ministry" unto the Lord.

Dr. Shon Neyland, Senior Pastor
Highland Christian Center, Portland, Oregon
Colonel, U.S. Air Force (Ret.)

Contents

PREFACE

Fifty years is a long time to be in the ministry. Fifty years is a long time for anything! A lot can happen in half a century, some good and some bad, but that's not the way I was looking at it when I got started.

I expected good. I mean, if you love the Lord, read the Bible, pray, have enough faith, and don't do anything too bad, things ought to go pretty well for you, don't you think?

And at times they did.

I've been privileged to serve in four Christian organizations: Cru (Campus Crusade for Christ when I was on staff), Club Beyond (Young Life's military branch), and two Protestant denominations. I started by working in campus ministry at several different universities and those were good years. Not that everything always went smoothly, but sharing Christ, making disciples and building a movement were exciting.

After three years directing a ministry at one school in the Midwest, where we saw significant success, I moved on to a different university in the Northeast. At a meeting of other ministry staff from the area, I was introduced as "a legend in the ministry." Wow, I've got to admit that felt awfully good!

Three years later I was fired.

I'll tell that story in a bit, but suffice to say, that did not feel so good. In fact, it hurt so much I wanted to quit the ministry for good and do something else. Anything else.

That's why I'm writing this book. My experience, along with that of many, many others whom I've known, has been that ministry hurts. It can hurt often and it can hurt badly. And when I'm using the term "ministry," I'm referring to a wide range of Christian service, including full-time or vocational service such as pastor or other church staff, Christian counselor, missionary, parachurch staff, and employees at all kinds of Christian organizations. If any of those settings are where you've been serving, you will probably be able to identify with some of these stories.

But I'm also talking about non-paid volunteer ministry: serving on a church board, teaching Sunday School, leading a youth group, teaching a Bible study, helping with a ministry like Young Life or Youth for Christ, volunteering in a pro-life ministry or at a Christian homeless shelter, and on and on it goes. There are any number of ways to serve Christ and others. Ministry doesn't have to be full-time or paid to be hurtful.

Don't get me wrong. Although I'm saying that ministry can be a painful experience, there's no doubt that it can also be joyous and exciting, satisfying and good.

Let's put it this way: if you feel good all day long, except for a migraine headache from 3pm to 5pm in the afternoon, what do you think you'll remember most about that day? Chances are pretty good it will be those two hours of misery.

So it also can be with ministry, and if you don't believe me, just take a quick look back at Elijah in the Old Testament. Remember when he had that fantastic head-to-head duel with the several hundred prophets of Baal? Remember how God answered his call in the most dramatic way possible by sending fire on his water-logged altar and proving once and for all that the God of Israel reigned over all others? What an unbelievable victory and an exhilarating high point of ministry for Elijah. Now that man was indeed a legend!

Then, before he knew it, Elijah was running for the hills because he'd heard a little threat from nasty old Queen Jezebel that she was coming to get him. This statement in 1 Kings 19:4 is almost too much to believe but here's what happened next: *Elijah came to a broom tree, sat down under it and prayed that he might die. "I have had enough, Lord," he said. "Take my life; I am no better than my ancestors."*

Wow. You talk about ups and downs in ministry? It doesn't get much more down than that. Elijah had had it, he wanted to quit --- he even wanted to die.

That's the nature of ministry, though. It can hurt. It can disappoint. It can leave you worn out, frazzled, discouraged, and wanting to quit, and most people in ministry have been there.

You might be there right now.

Through the chapters of this book, you'll see that reality both in Scripture and in anecdotes from the lives of many people in ministry today. And that will include me, because all these years in Christian work have given me a chance to see, if not all, certainly a lot.

Don't think, however, that's the final word on ministry. Not at all. You're going to see the other side of all this, too, the value and the privilege and the lasting worth of serving the Lord and working with people.

The Apostle Paul knew more than his share of suffering in serving Christ and yet he said, *"I have fought the good fight, I have finished the race, I have kept the faith. Now there is in store for me the crown of righteousness, which the Lord, the righteous Judge, will award to me on that day –- and not only to me, but also to all who have longed for his appearing"* (2 Timothy 4:7-8).

Before we get there, though, we'll have to wade through a lot of the stuff that makes people in ministry wonder, "Why bother? Why put up with all this? This isn't what I signed up for." And there's no escaping it.

According to one study, just ten percent of those who go into pastoral ministry will end their careers as pastors. Of course, there may be many reasons why that is so, including many good reasons that take them in another direction. Without question, though, one of the main reasons for leaving ministry is the pain, the hurt and the disappointment that are inherent in ministry.

So what will keep you going through the tougher times of ministry? What will keep you from quitting?

The Incline is a Colorado landmark and it's a rite of passage for those who think they're ready to tackle one of Colorado's "14ers" (mountains over 14,000 feet in elevation).

Located by Pike's Peak in Manitou Springs, the Incline follows an old, narrow-gauge railway line that washed out a number of years ago. The hike is just .88 miles in length. Pretty easy, right? But in that less-than-a-mile stretch, you'll walk up 2,744 steps, gaining over 2,000 feet in elevation to end at 8,590 feet, and you'll do so on a slope that averages a 41% grade with a top grade of 68% at one point. I don't care where you come from, that's steep!

The first time I tackled it was when we were living in Nebraska and out visiting friends in Colorado Springs. My friend suggested we do it and I figured, *why not, I'm in good shape, used to running several miles a day, so a little hike of less than a mile shouldn't be too bad*. Somebody mentioned something about needing to acclimate to the altitude, but where we lived in Nebraska was 1440 feet above sea level so it wasn't as though I was coming from zero altitude. And yes, it was going to be 85 degrees that day, but that would just loosen up the old joints.

So off we went the next morning. The first hundred yards were a piece of cake. The next hundred felt like the cake was starting to clog my lungs. And the rest of the way felt like the cake had metastasized in my stomach, my lungs and every other body part. Wow, had I underestimated what this took.

About halfway up I was ready to pack it in. I really didn't think I was going to make it or could make it. There's a main bailout point at about that level and I came sooooooo close to taking it. From there it would have been a leisurely walk down the Barr Trail to the parking lot, where I could hear my car calling my name! The only thing that kept me going was knowing, if I did bail out and for the rest of my life, I would never hear the end of it from my friend.

So I kept going. And I made it. Of course, I was sick for the rest of the day, but I made it. And despite the sickness, I felt fantastic. Hanging in there and accomplishing something challenging like that will do that for you.

What will keep you going? How will you make it to the finish line? And I don't mean just your present ministry, I mean overall. Despite any things that have happened to you in serving the Lord, despite the challenges, heartaches, frustrations, failures and pain, will you be there at the end, still loving the Lord and loving others?

So let's take a look at why ministry hurts and how to survive when it does. Some true stories, both mine and others', some tears, some laughs, some, "you've got to be kidding me!" moments … and some perspective from the Lord that I think can make a huge difference.

And we might as well start with one of the worst things that ever happened to me in all my time in ministry.

01

BUTTING HEADS

I got fired.

That's right, a dedicated Christian worker (that's me!) was terminated by another dedicated Christian worker (my boss).

We were both in our late 20s, working in a campus ministry. I directed the program at a university in New England; he supervised the group of directors working at a number of schools in the area.

I was the good guy and he was the bad guy. Hey, I'm writing this book and when he writes his own, he can turn that around.

Actually, we were both the dumb guys!

Here's how this played out. I'd been doing my job for six years and had had at least some degree of success.

Will Sanborn

I've never been the most self-confident guy, but I loved working with college students and I did feel like I knew what I was doing.

Then he became my supervisor. He was cocky, self-assured, younger than most of us, and he wanted to stamp his style on all of us under his leadership. *Uh-oh, is my bias showing through again?*

Really, he was a very talented person, motivated, capable and with a good heart for seeing all these campus ministries thrive. It was just that he and I didn't mesh well personally.

It might have been our competitiveness. Take one example: We both loved playing flag football. At our annual fall retreat for all the campus staff in our area, we would play a flag football game --- a team of campus directors led by me and a team of other staff members led by him. He played quarterback for his team and I was the QB for mine.

The first time we played, his team smoked our team, and of course, being the cocky self-assured guy he was, he rubbed that in for the rest of the retreat.

My response? I stewed over it. I planned, strategized, schemed and plotted how I would turn things around the next year. I diagrammed the plays we would use and drew out the defensive scheme to shut down their offense.

And we did it. When we played the game at the next fall retreat, we won going away. I felt great as all the plays I had devised over the past year worked and we suffocated their offense like we were the 1986 Chicago Bears.

His response? I don't think he was too happy about it.

So that's just a little backdrop of what led to my being fired. That same competitiveness that fueled our football rivalry fueled our ministry rivalry as well. I thought I knew better than him; he thought he knew better than me. He didn't value my abilities as much as I would have wanted him to, and I didn't respect and accept his leadership like I should have.

We were like two bighorn sheep butting heads. Not much sense to it, not much was accomplished, but we did it anyway.

It all came to a head when I balked at following through on an assignment he gave me. I didn't agree with it and I told him so. He told me that was it, he'd had it with my negative attitude. I was terminated --- right then and there, dismissed from the ministry, effective immediately.

That floored me. I had no inkling that was coming. Even if I had, I would never have believed it was possible. You know the old saw about how, in a crisis or tough time, your life flashes before your eyes? Well, that's about what happened. I pictured having to tell my wife I'd just lost my job. How would I explain it to my staff team and the students? What about having to let my financial supporters know that I'd been kicked out the door?

Can you hold on for a bit to find out how that ended? Let's back up a minute and examine why it happened. Among the many reasons why ministry hurts and causes pain, not the least of them is our own sin.

Will Sanborn

THE ATTITUDES BEHIND THE ACTIONS

I was a sinner and he was a sinner. It doesn't really matter which one of us was the bigger sinner, it only matters that we both were sinners. And without a doubt, sin brings problems, conflict, hurt and pain.

I thought I knew more than he did. I thought I was more qualified than he was (a doubtful conclusion). Again, it doesn't really matter whether I was right or wrong about that because I was wrong not to accept and respect his leadership. God had placed him in that role and my stubborn negativity created an unhealthy relationship right from the start. It hurt terribly when it all blew up in my face, but I was the one who had set it all in motion.

I don't think I was ready to fully admit that back then. I was too immature, a little too full of myself and a little too ready to put the blame on someone else rather than to see my own responsibility.

But that's what immaturity does. It blames others, someone else, something else, anything other than yourself.

I was about five years old when I did one of the dumber things I've ever done, but at least I can blame this one on my youth. My dad would often come home for lunch from his job, and on this summer day, as he drove out of the driveway and up the street, I playfully pretended to be pushing the car. Fun stuff, except for some strange reason I didn't let go. I held onto the back bumper as I fell on my knees. A hundred yards or so of that tore up my knees pretty good before I finally let go of the car.

Now who was at fault for my injuries? Well, it would be easy enough to blame my dad. He should have looked back and noticed that I was "pushing" the car. He should have realized that I hadn't let go and that I was dragging on my knees, and the least he could have done was stop the car and get out and apologize. Of course, he hadn't even seen what had happened and he drove away without an inkling of the damage done.

Blaming him would have gotten everything turned around. There really was only one person to blame and that was me. I'm the one who foolishly played around with a moving vehicle. I'm the one who held on, even when my knees were being shredded. I'm the one who caused the damage.

I think before we get too far into our look at why ministry can hurt so much, it's not a bad idea to admit early on that sometimes we're the problem. Sometimes, we're the ones who cause the damage. I know you remember what Jesus said, *"Why do you look at the speck of sawdust in your brother's eye and pay no attention to the plank in your own eye?"* (Matthew 7:3)

The old spiritual says, "It's me, it's me, it's me, O Lord, standing in the need of prayer. Not my brother, not my sister, but it's me, O Lord, standing in the need of prayer." That's a healthy song to sing every so often, especially when you might be steaming over how someone has done you wrong.

But having said that, let's be clear: there are often times in ministry when you have done nothing wrong, nothing to deserve the unfair treatment you receive. One of the hardest things you face is when you suffer for no good reason at all.

HE DID NOTHING WRONG

Let's close this chapter with one striking example of that from Scripture.

John the Baptist was as good as they come, a spiritual giant, someone Jesus described as the greatest of men born from a woman. His ministry was to be the forerunner, the introducer of the Messiah, and he did it extremely well. He was faithful, determined, strong, capable and successful. He did exactly what God had called him to do.

And yet his reward, on earth, at least, was so horrible it defies description. I'll summarize it here but you would do well to read it again in Matthew 14.

Herod Antipas resented John because John had criticized Herod's actions in stealing his brother's wife and marrying her. Although he would just as soon have killed John right away, Herod put him in prison so as not to rile up the Baptist's followers.

Sometime later, during Herod's birthday party, one at which Herod and his guests were likely drinking heavily, his stepdaughter danced in a way that so pleased Herod he promised her, on oath, to reward her with whatever she wanted. After conferring with her mom, Herod's ill-gotten wife, she came back with this gruesome request: "*Give me here on a platter the head of John the Baptist.*"

Ugh. Now stop for a minute. Could this really be happening? Could the wicked whim of a teenage girl and her evil mom actually result in the senseless death of this great man of God? If you made a list of all those who have served well in ministry over the centuries, who were faithful to God, and who excelled in what they did, where would John rank? Top ten? Top three? Maybe the best ever?

And yet this was the reward for his service. What a travesty.

If someone of John's godliness faced that degree of injustice for his faithful ministry, should it be any surprise that for you and me, ministry sometimes will hurt and hurt bad?

Are you wondering whatever happened between me and my supervisor? Well, it was a mix. We talked it through right then and there, and he rescinded his termination declaration. We made a little progress as we talked, and we ended in prayer and a handshake. Honestly, it was a less-than-satisfactory resolution; it was more like a practical truce that at least saw us through the rest of the year peaceably. If I were able to relive those couple years under his leadership, I would hope with the maturity I've gained since then that I would do a much better job. And I would hope the same for him.

ONE MORE THING

Even though you're likely very familiar with the story of John the Baptist, it's worth a little more thought. Check out Matthew 11:1-19 and 14:1-12. Read it over and then see what you think:

- Why do you think God allowed John's life to end the way it did?

- How could such a nasty, cruel, ungodly family like Herod Antipas, his wife and his stepdaughter succeed in destroying such a godly man as John?

- What do you think John was thinking as he waited in prison and then as he learned his fate?

- And what do you think it was like for John at the moment he entered into God's presence?

- Now think of a time in your own ministry when you were treated unfairly and suffered through no fault of your own. How did you handle it? Why do you think God allows painful and unfair things like that in your own life?

02

GREAT EXPECTATIONS

Now this was the way to start a new year. The Christian organization I was working for scheduled its national staff conference for the first week of January. In Florida. On Disney property. What could be better than that, leaving the frozen north for the warm south, Mickey and Minnie, Splash Mountain and Pirates of the Caribbean? Except …

Except that getting ready to leave our house for the airport, somehow — I don't remember just how it happened other than that I was rushing like crazy to be on time for our flight — but whatever, somehow, I managed to drop my cell phone in the toilet. No, I don't know how I managed to do that and yes, my wife has already asked me that question, one thousand two hundred times, in fact!

Anyway, I fished it out as quickly as I could, but it was too late. Despite my desperate attempts at resuscitation, including the fail-safe stick-it-in-a-bowl-of-rice method, it was dead. There would be no chance to replace it while at Disney World, so a week without a cell phone. What a dork.

It gets better. On the first flight, I was shuffling down the aisle looking for my seat number. As I leaned in to see the number on the overhead bin, somehow -- no, I don't remember just how this happened either -- but whatever. Somehow, I managed to bang my forehead on the metal seat number, and before I knew it, I was bleeding all over the place. A multitude of band aids, wet paper towels and pressure eventually staunched the flow. But for the rest of the week, I had to explain over and over, to countless people, why I had a big band aid on my forehead, why I didn't have a cell phone, and why I was such a big, double dork!

Great expectations can become great disappointments in the blink of an eye. So it goes in the ministry. I'm guessing that whatever kind of ministry you've been in, you went into it with a desire to serve the Lord and with the hope of seeing him use you in people's lives. I mean, why else would you do it?

But I'm guessing, too, that as time went on, those expectations weren't always realized. I hope they have for you, but my own experience, the experience of many others and the messages of Scripture, would suggest otherwise.

Every situation is unique, of course, but in most cases of disappointment, one or more of these factors are involved:

- our own sins
- other people's sins
- the effects of a sin-riddled world
- the efforts of the enemy

Without question, life is hard. So why wouldn't ministry be? I've had the adventure of climbing Pike's Peak several times with my youngest son. Fantastic feeling to reach the summit, but it hasn't always been a fantastic feeling along the way. My most common physical position has been bending over and putting my hands on my knees. *Breathe, Will, breathe!*

Ministry is something like that. It can be exciting and fulfilling but there are bound to be times when you wonder if it's worth it and if you can make it.

So why are we so surprised when troubles, difficulties, letdowns, and failures intrude on the desires, plans, and dreams of our ministry? Really, the issue isn't so much that we will have troubles, it's whether or not we'll keep on going despite those troubles.

THE EASY PART IS SETTING THE GOAL

Many years ago, I had the privilege of taking part in an incredible event, Explo '72 in Dallas, Texas. Campus Crusade for Christ (now known as Cru) envisioned, planned and carried out this weeklong conference for high school and college students. The goal was to bring 100,000 students to Dallas for training and motivation to bring about an explosion of evangelism throughout the United States and around the world.

What a fantastic vision, but what an overwhelming challenge. As one of the conference's main leaders put it in the understatement of the year, "The logistics of putting on a conference of this size are immense."

Months and months and more months went into the preparation for this event. Can you imagine what all that would entail? Promoting, recruiting, transporting, housing, feeding, training, protecting, scheduling, praying, financing …. add a dozen more areas and you still haven't covered all the logistics.

As one of the several thousand staff members tasked with accomplishing those things, I learned a lot about how ministry expectations can easily be drowned in the realities of the work. One staff member wisecracked, "We began by praying for REVIVAL; we ended up praying for SURVIVAL!"

Explo '72 ended up drawing "only" about 85,000 students, and no doubt it took a toll on those who planned and staffed it, but what a fantastic week of spiritual vision and accomplishment that changed many, many lives.

For me, it brought an indelible lesson: the easier part of ministry is imagining the goal, the harder part is getting there.

Great expectations for a ministry are indeed great. Honestly, we shouldn't be serving in ministry if we don't have a desire for and an expectation that God will use us to make a difference in lives, whether a huge difference or just a little bitty one. The challenge comes when those troubles that Jesus mentioned show up. When ministry doesn't go the way you had envisioned, when you realize you're not as ready for it as you thought you were, when others you thought were your allies somehow have become your opponents, what do you do then?

EXPECTATIONS GIVE WAY TO REALITY

Will you give me a little leeway with a Biblical example? Follow me to Revelation 11, where John gives the account of the two witnesses. There's so much more here than we will deal with, but here's the gist of it:

The Apostle John had been given a vision of end-time events, and chapter by chapter he's been laying out the things leading to the triumphant return of Jesus Christ. In Chapter 11, he describes the actions of the two unnamed witnesses who stand in the temple in Jerusalem to prophesy God's message to the world.

They do so for 1,260 days amounting to 30 months or 3½ years. And what a ministry they have for that period! Here's how John describes it:

These are the two olive trees and the two lampstands that stand before the Lord of the earth. If anyone tries to harm them, fire comes from their mouths and devours their enemies. This is how anyone who wants to harm them must die. These men have power to shut up the sky so that it will not rain during the time they are prophesying; and they have power to turn the waters into blood and to strike the earth with every kind of plague as often as they want. (11:3—6)

Wow, that's awesome. That's the way ministry ought to go, isn't it? You declare God's Word and people take notice; nothing can stand in your way. That would be some kind of church!

Now I asked you to give me a little leeway on this and here's why. Let me give a fanciful recounting of this that puts us into it --- and trust me, I know this is not good biblical exposition, but bear with me:

Suppose you were one of those witnesses and that was your ministry for those three-and-a-half years. You'd be feeling pretty good about it, wouldn't you? I mean, you're drawing huge crowds and they just keep coming, day after day. You're banging out God's Word to all those people and nobody dares to stop you. You are a major success. This is even better than you had ever dared dream about. You're unstoppable. Why, God's even using you to do miracles. You're getting booked for conference gigs all over the place, plus a book tour, and you're planning temple renovations that would make Solomon jealous.

You, my friend, have made it big. Not only have you realized all your expectations and dreams, but now they have expanded. There's no stopping you now. You are a faithful servant of God and God is using you big time. Ministry is everything you had hoped it would be, and more!

But you've read Revelation 11 before, haven't you? You know what's coming next and it's not pretty:

Now when they have finished their testimony, the beast that comes up from the Abyss will attack them, and overpower and kill them. Their bodies will lie in the street of the great city, which is figuratively called Sodom and Egypt, where also their Lord was crucified. For three and a half days, men from every people, tribe, language and nation will gaze on their bodies and refuse them burial. The inhabitants of the earth will gloat over them and will celebrate by sending each other gifts, because these

*two prophets had tormented those who live on the earth.
(11:7—10)*

Whoa, wait a minute. That's not the way we would
have written it. Let's keep going with this fanciful way of
putting us into this account. Now after three-and-a-half
years of unparalleled ministry success, the bottom drops
out. Not only are you no longer proclaiming God's Word
with no one daring to challenge you, but now you're dead.

And not just regular dead. This Beast comes out of
nowhere and attacks and kills you. No one defends you,
no one jumps in to rescue you, not even God himself
does anything to help. You are dead.

And disgracefully dead. Your body just lies there in
the street as people gloat over it. Three-and-a-half days
go by, no funeral, no preparation of the body, it just
sprawls there in disgrace and humiliation.

Not a pretty sight, huh? So how would you be
feeling about that? I mean right before you died, because
it would be hard to do much thinking about it while you
were lying there in the street dead. Would you think
something like, "Uh, God, how could you let this
happen? I've been serving you for more than three years,
doing everything you asked of me, and this is how you
treat me? This is what I get for being faithful? What kind
of deal is that?"

Now let's come back to a more proper biblical
interpretation. Obviously, this passage is not describing
you or me. These are end-time events that will happen,
and these two witnesses will do as John described as part
of God's judgment on the world shortly before the return
of Christ. As you know, if you've read this before, God

does step in after the three-and-a-half days and he brings these two witnesses back to life, then takes them into heaven with him. What a striking picture of spiritual reality as God's enemies can never, and will never, prevail in the end against God and his church.

Back to us now. I'm saying here that one of our challenges and stumbling blocks in ministry is expecting that because we are serving Christ, things ought to go well for us. Everyone should appreciate what we do. There should be a really good response to our ministry. Maybe we won't make a ton of money, but there ought to be respect and appreciation, gratitude and success, and hey, some material reward shouldn't be out of the question, either.

In other words, God ought to reward us, here and now, for serving him. We probably wouldn't come out and say it quite that way, but down deep, that's what we think. Our expectation is that when we serve God, he ought to treat us right. It's only fair.

When he doesn't treat us fairly, when ministry doesn't go the way we want it to go, we are disappointed, not just in our ministry but in God. So many others seem to have a lot of success in ministry; God's blessing them it seems, so why isn't he coming through for us?

It's awfully easy for ministry to turn sour. There are lots of reasons for that, but one reason, maybe even a main reason, is that we may have unrealistic (read: unbiblical) expectations of serving God.

Jesus laid out the expectations for his disciples in John 16:33, "*I have told you these things, so that in me you may have peace.* **In this world you will have trouble.** *But take heart! I have overcome the world.*" (emphasis added)

ONE MORE THING

- What kinds of troubles do you think Jesus had in mind when he said this?

- What kinds of troubles have you faced in your ministries?

- How are you doing on the "take heart" part? Has that been winning for you, or has it been "the troubles"?

- What else can you take away from that passage about the two witnesses?

03

WHEN PEOPLE LET YOU DOWN

And I thought I had it bad.

Tullian Tchividjian is a pastor who knows something of the "ouch" of ministry. In an interview in *Leadership Journal*, he shared some of those experiences, starting when he was asked to follow a well-known pastor in a very large church when that pastor retired. Within seven months, a petition (led by the former pastor's daughter!) demanding Tchividjian resign circulated through the congregation. Thankfully, it failed to remove him but that wasn't the end of it.

The unhappy segment of the church would put petitions on cars out in the parking lot during worship services. Anonymous blogs and letters added to the tension. Here's how Tchividjian described the atmosphere in church during that time:

"It was tremendously uncomfortable coming to worship every Sunday morning during that time not knowing who liked you and who hated you. There were people in the choir who, when I would stand up to preach, would get up and walk out. People would grab me in the hallway between services and say, 'You're ruining this church, and I'm going to do everything I can to stop you.' I would come out to my car and it would be keyed."[1]

Ministry is tough enough when there's opposition out in the unbelieving community, but when it's inside your own group, it's so much worse. You question why God doesn't make things a little easier for people who faithfully serve him (like you!), and then it gets even worse when you're let down or attacked by people you're trying to help (like them!).

JOB'S FRIENDS

Job's case in the Old Testament is a classic example so let's take a look. Not too deep, not too long; there are countless Bible teachers far more capable than I who have expounded on the truths of this book over the centuries. For our purposes, let's just do a brief overview.

Job lived through everything we're considering and more:

- Job was a godly man, far more godly than most of us.

- He was very wealthy and had a large family.

---

[1] Leadership Journal, Fall 2011, p. 23

- By all appearances he was greatly blessed by God and extremely fortunate.

- Until …. with no warning and with no discernible cause (at least so far as Job knew), the bottom fell out.

- An enemy attacked and stole Job's donkeys and oxen, killing his servants who attended them.

- Lightning struck and killed Job's sheep along with the shepherds.

- Another enemy made off with his camels after murdering those in charge of them.

- Finally, while Job's seven sons and three daughters were celebrating with a meal at the oldest brother's house, a fierce windstorm caused the house to collapse on them, killing them all.

Good grief, stop the story for a minute and just take in what has happened: Job's entire world has fallen apart. His possessions have been decimated. His wealth is gone. His family, with the exception of his wife, is no more. Can you imagine how he felt? Can you even begin to put yourself in his place?

Now, if you are familiar with the account, you know that behind all that happened stood Satan, who had challenged God concerning God's servant Job. But Job didn't know that. In fact, so far as we can see, God never did tell Job about the spiritual battle behind the events. All Job had to go on was his belief that God was good, and that God was to be worshiped and trusted.

You also know that the story wasn't over. When Job responded in trusting worship of God, Satan upped the ante and protested that Job would curse God if his own health was taken from him. God allowed him to do so but excepting that Job's life could not be taken. Here's what followed:

- Satan afflicted Job with painful sores over his entire body, from the bottom of his feet to the top of his head.

- As the book unfolds, Job describes the extent of this sickness as including festering sores, scabs that peeled and turned black, an appearance so appalling that it shocked and disgusted others, bad breath, fever, boils and who knows what else!

- Job's wife, his only remaining family, told him to give up, curse this horrible God and die. *Hey, thanks, for the encouragement, Hon!*

Somehow, after all this, Job was still standing. He refused to curse God. And how he answered his wife has to make the Faith Hall of Fame: "Shall we accept good from God, and not trouble?"

Hard to believe, but even so, his suffering still wasn't over. When he desperately needed some understanding, encouragement and help, his three friends showed up: Eliphaz, Bildad and Zophar. And give credit where credit is due; for an entire week they sat quietly with him, just being there for him as they joined in his sorrowful weeping. Good for them. You couldn't have asked for anything more.

Regrettably, though, they hung around. If they had only headed home after that first week! Instead, they stayed and began to analyze the situation. In short, their logic went like this:

A. God is good and gives good things to those who love him and he rains punishment on those who oppose him.

B. Job was obviously being punished by God.

C. Therefore, Job must be evil and deserving of all this punishment.

So much for comforting the afflicted. They were Job's last best hope after he had lost his wealth, his possessions, his children and even the loyal love of his wife.

Now stop here for another moment. You know that the end of the account is going to be fantastic. God is going to bless Job more than ever before --- although don't forget that the sufferings he endured, including the loss of his ten children, could never be erased.

But right now, when he needed it the most, from the people he most needed it, no help was coming. His wife and his best friends let Job down. Talk about rubbing salt into his wounds.

YOUR FRIENDS

Have you ever felt that way? Ever feel like when you most needed encouragement from people who've given just the opposite? You've ministered to people and you thought they were your friends, but when the chips were down, friends were nowhere to be found?

One person was leading an adult Bible study group in his church. Along with the study, the goal was to encourage and care for one another, all of which sounded great …. on paper. The leader was there for people when things were going badly in their lives and he felt there was some healthy spiritual depth growing in the group.

Then something turned that upside down. That small group leader found himself in an uncomfortable and tense situation with another leader in the church, someone who was higher up the ladder in standing and influence, as they disagreed over a significant issue. The issue festered and, as so often happens, people in the church began taking sides. The Bible study leader reluctantly decided to leave the church because of the situation.

Those things happen in churches much more often than you'd like them to, but something else happened that left a deep scar on his spirit. His caring group didn't care. The people he had worked with, cared for and helped through their own difficult situations abandoned him. Maybe it was because they didn't want to get on the wrong side of that other higher-up leader; maybe it was because they didn't know what to do; maybe they didn't want to make matters worse. Whatever it was, they weren't there when he needed them the most. He has never really trusted a small group again.

A very good friend of mine recounts her own experience. She and her husband were serving in full-time ministry and were active in their local church. She took charge of the children's ministry, including supervising the volunteers who helped. One high school student was especially helpful. He worked with the four- and five-year-olds and was the kind of young man everyone considered wonderful.

It turned out he wasn't. This was long before background checks became commonplace in churches. Church leaders back then tended to assume good motives from people who volunteered. Eventually, it came to light that he had improperly touched a little girl while alone with her. He had gotten bolder as time went on, and for several years, he had molested other young children in the church.

It shook the church to its core. The church split, pastors left, people formed a support group to help those who had been hurt by his actions. In all that, however, my friend and her husband were left out. Many people assumed that she must have known what was happening and had done nothing about it. Nothing could have been farther from the truth, but truth doesn't always win out in these situations, does it?

The implications and the rejection soon pushed them out of the church, and the repercussions lasted much longer. In the next church they joined, it was difficult for them to trust the leadership and to feel secure with the people with whom they worshiped. Being misjudged and misunderstood by fellow believers, ones you think knew you well and trusted you, is a bitter pill. As my friend put it, "Pain is just a heartbeat away for each of us."

Job knew that pain. So did others in the Bible.

Paul knew it. In 2 Timothy 4, he says *"Demas, because he loved this world, has deserted me …. Alexander the metalworker did me a great deal of harm …. at my first defense, no one came to my support, but everyone deserted me."*

John knew it. In 3 John he writes, *"Diotrephes, who loves to be first, will have nothing to do with us. So if I come, I will call attention to what he is doing, gossiping maliciously about us."*

Jesus knew it. In Mark 14, as he neared the cross, he said, *"You will all fall away, for it is written, 'I will strike the shepherd and the sheep will be scattered.'"*

When Peter protested that he would never do that, Jesus responded, *"I tell you the truth, today – yes, tonight – before the rooster crows twice you yourself will disown me three times."*

And soon after, in deep distress as he prayed in Gethsemane, his disciples, when he needed them the most, fell asleep. Jesus asked, *"Simon, are you asleep? Could you not keep watch for one hour?"*

You know that pain, too.

ONE MORE THING

Two questions to think about:

- When others you trust let you down, how do you handle it?

- How are you doing in being there when others need you?

04

COMPARISON SHOPPING

One of the best books I read when I was a pastor was "Liberating Ministry from the Success Syndrome," by Kent and Barbara Hughes. It described Kent's experiences pastoring a small church and how he used to judge his success (or lack thereof) by the numbers: how many people came to church. Was it more or less than the year before? How was the budget doing? How did the people treat him? How did his church compare to others he knew, etc., etc., etc. His premise was that all those things were the wrong criteria for evaluating success in ministry.

It's an excellent book, well worth reading. Their insights are spot on and helpful.

It's also one of the worst books I've read. Well, not really, but by the time he wrote the book he had become a "successful" pastor; that is, he led a large congregation, he wrote a best-selling book, he spoke at conferences around the world.

So yes, yes, a hundred timcs yes, I agree with his premise that numbers and growth are really not the measuring stick for success in ministry. However, I'd say that many, if not most, of us still play the numbers game.

I know a pastor of a smaller church who noticed something very unusual going on in the parking lot one weekday morning. There was a sizable group of people holding cell phones and just kind of buzzing around here and there. Eventually, they went away and he forgot about it. Then a few days later, another group showed up doing the same thing before leaving. Puzzled, he mentioned it to a friend and finally got the answer as to what was going on. Somehow the church parking lot had become a local Pokémon™ hot spot, or "Poke Stop," where players gathered to play the game. Crazy stuff, but I wondered …. I mean, **he** wondered, that pastor, not me, if he could count those people in the weekly worship attendance numbers to boost the average!

Okay, I realize I'm being just a little cynical here. Cynicism, however, often carries a strong whiff of truth. Those in Christian work know that in God's eyes success is measured by things such as character, faithfulness, loving God and loving others. Those same people in Christian work know that in people's eyes it is measured by numbers: how many people, how much money, how much influence, how much recognition.

So after reading that book, guess who still felt like a failure? That would be me.

You know why? Because I thought, *sure, it's easy for them to talk about their past experiences when they struggled with feeling like a failure. But now they're a big-time success.*

And I'm not.

Yes, I recognize my jealousy and pettiness. But at least give me a couple points for honesty! I'm guessing, if you're being honest, you've felt this same way, too. Whatever kind of ministry you do, it is so easy to compare yourself to others and feel like you're coming up short. We know we should rejoice with those who rejoice, but it's not always easy, is it? Not when you feel you have little to rejoice about yourself.

What if you go through a whole career and never reach that level where others look at you as someone who really succeeded? No trophies, no best-selling book, no invitations to address a conference or convention, no banquets in your honor.

Here's an undocumented, best-guess estimate of how many people serving the Lord in one way or another never get to the point of great success and fame: **MOST OF THEM!**

And that likely includes you. It certainly includes me.

Let's use churches as our ministry checkpoint, so consider some of these statistics:

- there are about 350,000 churches in the United States

- the median size of a church (that is, how many people attend each Sunday) is 75

- 60% of churches average less than 100 people in attendance at weekend services

- half of all people who attend churches in the U.S. go to the top 10% of churches

- only about 20% of the U.S. population attend church with any degree of regularity

Statistics like these should be taken with a grain of salt as they are always changing from year to year. Still, they certainly give at least a glimpse into why it is so easy for those in ministry to feel like they are failures. Most churches, and most other types of ministries, are relatively small. If you're a pastor, chances are you have less than 100 people out on a Sunday morning. If you're in a parachurch ministry, say on a high school or college campus, chances are that you are nowhere near the biggest or most popular group on campus.

As a pastor, I could always console myself with reasons why our church wasn't bigger than it was. I saw one compilation of excuses people made for not attending church:

- "The church is too close to drive and too far to walk."

- "I always get hemorrhoids on Sundays."

- "My wife cooked bacon for breakfast and now all our clothes smell like bacon."

- "The pastor is too attractive. When I see him preaching, I have impure thoughts and I am distracted." (Now I'm pretty sure that must have been the reason why my church wasn't bigger than it was!)

So let's do a little comparison shopping through the Bible to see who was a success and who was a failure.

COMPARISON #1

In the church at Antioch there were prophets and teachers: Barnabas, Simeon called Niger, Lucius of Cyrene, Manaen (who had been brought up with Herod the Tetrarch) and Saul. While they were worshiping the Lord and fasting, the Holy Spirit said, "Set apart for me Barnabas and Saul for the work to which I have called them. So after they had fasted and prayed, they placed their hands on them and sent them off." (Acts 13:1)

You've probably heard of Barnabas and Saul, who was soon to become known as Paul. Paul was on his way to becoming the megachurch pastor, the preacher everyone wanted to hear, the conference speaker, the world traveler, the best-selling author. After all, he did write 13 books of the New Testament.

Barnabas was pretty well-known, too. Although he played second fiddle to Paul, he was quite the leader in his own right. He's the one who mentored Paul early on and helped set the stage for Paul's successful ministry. If I were comparing what he did then to what we're accustomed to now, I'd label him as the executive pastor of a megachurch, not the lead man, but someone everyone else recognized as vital to the overall operation.

So you know those two. But the other guys? Niger, Lucius, Manaen? I'd be willing to bet that not one in a hundred Christians today could identify who they were and what they did. Do you think they ever felt like failures, compared to the big two with whom they were associated? They'd be like the couple who hold a little Bible study in their home on a Thursday evening, which, on a good week, draws maybe six or seven people. Turn on the TV and you can watch some well-known Christian personality teaching the exact same passage, but with an audience in the millions. Is that couple significant or would it just be the star on the screen?

COMPARISON #2

We've already had a brief look at Elijah. Even with that bout of depression, we know what a winner he was… the great prophet, doer of unbelievable miracles, the guy who stood up to King Ahab and all the false prophets. He even raised somebody from the dead!

Then in 1 Kings 19 Elijah was struggling a bit and God encouraged him with these words in verse 18, *"Yet I reserve seven thousand in Israel – all whose knees have not bowed down to Baal and all whose mouths have not kissed him."*

So who were these people? I'll give a million dollars to anyone who can name all 7,000 of them. I'll give a million if you can name just seven of them! I think I'm on safe ground with this bet because they aren't named here or anywhere else. They were great believers, solid followers of the Lord who stayed true to him in desperate and dangerous times, but we don't even know their names.

I wonder how they felt as they watched Elijah's fame grow. Maybe a little jealous? Maybe a little bit put out by it? I hope not and I'm not accusing them of that, just wondering, because it's awfully easy to feel so little next to someone so big.

Oh, and I should mention that although we don't know their names, God certainly does.

COMPARISON #3

I love the Old Testament story of Gideon. He had his own confidence problems and struggled at times to get up and go when God called him to do something. But when he did, he did it up right!

In Judges 7, God gave Gideon the task of taking on a coalition of Midianites and Amalekites, an invading army who far outnumbered the Israelite forces. Gideon hesitated, hemmed and hawed, but finally was ready to go.

God had more in mind than just a victory over the enemy, though. God instructed Gideon to cut down the number of his troops so that when the victory came Israel wouldn't think it was all due to their skill and strength.

From the starting number of some 32,000 soldiers, God whittled it down to just 300 men... 300 going up against some 135,000 of the enemy. And they won! What a victory, one that would go down in the history books of Israel as one of the all-time greatest.

And Gideon was the man! Famous, honored, they even wanted to make him king. But what about those 300 men that marched into battle behind him? I'm looking and looking, and I just don't see their names anywhere.

No statues in their honor. No movement to make any of them king. So how about them? Think they did any comparison shopping where they felt like they were nothing because Gideon was the big something?

Hey, we could do this all day long. Most believers serving the Lord (whether in Bible times or in our times) do so in relative obscurity. A few stand out. The greater number don't. So is the conclusion that those who don't are failures? That only the big names are the successes?

I mentioned before that I've been comparing myself to other Christian servants for fifty years. You would think I'd have learned by now! Whether in church or parachurch ministry, my comparison-shopping habit has been very much a part of my life. Invariably, when I've done that, I've ended up depressed. It's funny, one pastor friend commented to me once that he could see I was comfortable in my own skin. That would be true to a degree, but not when I get caught up in this losing game. I know Satan had a hand in making me feel that way, but I hardly needed his help. That just comes naturally to me! Maybe growing up the youngest of five boys and usually coming up on the short end of things set me up for that lack of confidence. Regardless, comparison shopping has long been a thorn in my ministry side.

Now I don't want to overstate this. God does expect our best, our faithfulness, the use of the gifts and talents he's given us, our reliance on his Spirit and power and so forth. If we fail in those things, then we have failed and need to own up to it.

But if we serve the Lord faithfully, then how he uses our service is up to him. If some are Pauls or Elijahs or

Gideons, that doesn't make failures out of those who aren't. Not in God's eyes.

Our challenge is to give our best and to celebrate the success of God's other servants, even when they outshine us. I'll admit I haven't always done well in those two areas, and I'll probably struggle with both until the day God takes me home. But I know this: God knows my name and he knows yours and what a privilege it is to serve the King of Kings and to leave the evaluation to him.

ONE MORE THING

Read Matthew 22:34-40. If you insist on self-judging whether you're successful or not, then start and end right here with what Jesus says is the most important thing of all.

05

CAN'T WE ALL JUST GET ALONG?

It was year nine, my last one in college ministry, and I was working as a campus director (CD) at a major university. The way it was set up back then was to pair the CD with a female staff member to supervise the women's side of the ministry. That person was called a Senior Woman.

For my first five years as a CD, I'd been very fortunate to work with several exceptional Senior Women. In each case, we partnered well in the ministry and formed a good friendship on top of that. It was a pleasure to work with them and added a lot to the overall campus ministry.

Not so much this time.

It's not that she wasn't a good person or that she wasn't a good staff member. It was just that we didn't mesh. At all.

If I liked blue, she liked red. If I ordered Coke™, she ordered Pepsi™. If I set a direction for our ministry, she pretty much ignored it and set her own.

Now she was new at this, her first time at it, while I'd been around the block a time or two by then. Maybe it didn't help much that I saw it that way, that she was a rookie needing direction, because she certainly didn't see it that way herself.

As the year went on, the distance between us grew. We weren't enemies by any means, but we sure weren't friends either. That personal distance increasingly showed as a schism in our overall ministry. She and I weren't on the same page (or even the same book at times!) and the result was that the campus movement suffered.

Looking back, I don't know if I tried hard enough to make it work. I think I did in the early months through the fall, but by Christmastime, I had pretty much given up. So had she. I think we just settled for a superficial level of relationship so as to avoid conflict, but that doesn't cut it in being leadership partners for a Christian ministry.

We made it through the year and then moved on to new ministries. A few years later, I wrote her a letter apologizing for not having given my best effort as her director that year. I think I kind of expected (or at least hoped) that she would respond with a similar apology. Nope. Nothing at all. She just agreed with my apology that I hadn't done a good job!

MINISTRY TEAMS DON'T COME WITH A GUARANTEE

So, what do you do when you're in a ministry and you and some co-worker just don't get along? It could be open conflict or it might be behind-the-scenes simmering tension.

Whatever it is, you know it's no good.

What's that passage that believers love to quote but don't always love to do?

"A new command I give you: Love one another. As I have loved you, so you must love one another. By this all men will know that you are my disciples, if you love one another." (John 13:35)

A friend working in a different college ministry had a co-worker, an older lady, who gave every appearance of being an excellent partner in the program. She was good at what she did and she was walking with the Lord. It's just that she wasn't really walking with her team.

She began to skim off some of the students into another program, something that she was more committed to than the one she had signed up for. Slowly at first, then later more openly and aggressively, she undermined the ministry. Her co-workers had welcomed her participation early on, but as they began to realize what was happening, those relationships cooled. More than that, they began to shun her, to avoid her and to become openly antagonistic toward her. The deteriorating relationships between her and the rest of the team took a real toll on the overall ministry.

Will Sanborn

Chances are that if you've been in ministry for any length of time, you've been there. Christians don't always get along well. Sometimes, they don't get along at all. Whether it's personality differences, differing backgrounds, preferences, misunderstandings, doctrinal disagreements, immaturities, you name it --- we Christians have a very hard time living up to John 13:35.

I know this one's an old joke and a little long, so if you've heard it before, just skip over it and move on. But you might like it and it sure does fit what we're thinking about here:

Two guys had just met and as they got to talking, they discovered that they both were Christians.

The first guy asked, "Are you Protestant or Catholic?"

"Protestant," the second guy answered.

"Me, too," said the first. "What denomination?"

The other guy said, "I'm a Baptist."

"No kidding, so am I. Are you Northern Baptist or Southern Baptist?"

The second guy replied, "Northern."

"Wow, I am, too. So Northern Conservative Baptist or Northern Liberal Baptist?"

"I'm Northern Conservative Baptist."

"This is amazing," said the first guy. "Are you Northern Conservative Baptist Great Lakes Region, or Northern Conservative Baptist Eastern Region?"

The second guy came back, "Northern Conservative Baptist Great Lakes Region."

"We're going to be the best of friends, I can tell! Are you Northern Conservative Baptist Great Lakes Region Council of 1879, or Northern Conservative Baptist Great Lakes Region Council of 1912?"

The guy said, "I'm Northern Conservative Baptist Great Lakes Region Council of 1912."

To which the first guy exclaimed, "Then die, heretic!"

Funny stuff but it doesn't take much to divide believers as evidenced by the dismal track record of how often churches split. By one estimate there are some 40,000 different Christian denominations worldwide. Take a moment to let that one sink in. Even acknowledging that diversity can be a really good thing, that seems a little extreme.

I spent a few months one time as an informal interim pastor in a small church. The former pastor had left to start a new church --- same denomination --- just a few miles down the road. He took a number of people along with him, leaving his former small church a much smaller church. As I met with various members of the original church, I found that there seemed to be several key factors that led to the fracture:

- disagreements over music style

- strong-willed leaders on both sides

- differing philosophies of ministry

- they didn't like the same kind of music!

- even stronger-willed leaders

- intense disagreement over music styles!!

In other words, it didn't take much to blow the church up and to give the local community a vivid picture of believers negating Jesus' command to love one another. Amazingly, the original congregation folded a little later and the pastor who had left to form a new church brought his little group back to the original church building to start over again there. I hope I'm wrong, but with that kind of track record I'd rate the chances of that new/old church having a fruitful and growing ministry as one in a hundred at best.

RELATIONSHIPS SOMETIMES GO SOUTH

Among the most painful parts of Christian ministry are the relationships that sour, sputter and fall apart. You go into it thinking how wonderful it will be to work alongside other believers, united in your devotion to Christ and to the ministry he's called you together to do. Too often, you come out deflated and defeated.

So what goes wrong? No need to go too deep here. It's human nature. We're sinners, plain and simple. We may be redeemed sinners, but we're still sinners who battle a self-centered tendency that affects any and every relationship we have. And let's not forget that there is an enemy wholeheartedly devoted to his goal to steal, kill and destroy.

Put those two things together and it's amazing that some teams of Christians ever make it at all.

I read a study some time back of what overseas missionaries say were the most challenging and difficult aspects of their work. You'd think it might be the cultural

58

adjustments, the language barriers, the challenge of trying to communicate the gospel successfully, financial pressures or maybe just the loneliness of being away from home. Obstacles for sure, but overwhelmingly they said it was relating to the other missionaries they worked with.

One missionary couple related a particularly sad story. They were serving overseas paired with another couple. After a few months at their post, the first couple wrote to friends back home that what they missed the most, of all things, was peanut butter. They just couldn't come by anywhere they were stationed. In response, those friends sent them a boxful of jars of peanut butter. What a gift! They were delighted.

The other couple wasn't. In fact, they were angry. They felt that being missionaries involved and even demanded sacrifice and that this first couple was violating all the rules of being a good missionary! Trivial, you think? Well, the difference of opinion degenerated into a fierce division between the two couples, resulting in a fractured relationship that poisoned everything they did. It was so bad that when the first couple returned home a few years later at the end of their assignment, they swore they would never again serve as missionaries anywhere anytime. All because of a few jars of peanut butter.

Sometimes, it's great. You're working in a ministry alongside other Christians, and they become your best friends, lifelong friends. You're partners together in God's work, and it produces a depth of relationship you've rarely found elsewhere. Treasure it! I could write a list a chapter long of the truly wonderful people I've been honored to know and to work with. I wouldn't trade those experiences and relationships for anything in the world. Any examples I give in this book of difficult times pale in comparison to the memories I have of scores and scores and scores of all of them. What a gift they have been in my life.

But let's face it, sometimes ministry relationships can be a disaster. You don't see eye to eye, you don't get along, there's no sense of being a team, you don't feel cared for or appreciated, you're worn down by the conflict, and on and on it goes. No wonder Jesus gave that command to love one another because he knows that it doesn't always happen naturally. We often need a reminder and a push.

In one church, a new children's pastor joined the team. Eager, energetic and enthusiastic, she seemed just right for the position and for the team. Her own ministry was somewhat slow to develop, but at least she contributed in various ways that did help the church overall.

As several years went by, though, something seemed just a little off. She wasn't as enthusiastic as before. There was a growing disconnect between her and the lead pastor. Even the church board began to sense an edge in how she related to them and to other leaders.

Eventually, it came out that she had been talking with a small group of people in the church, sharing her unhappiness with them about the lead pastor and other leaders. She didn't agree with the direction of the ministry, and she felt the biblical teaching was too shallow and not deep enough.

Her backdoor complaints took their toll. Some people left the church, others joined in the complaining, casting a negative pall over the ministry. Opportunities were lost, people were hurt, and the ministry was damaged before she was finally asked to leave her position.

That scenario can be found in countless churches and parachurch ministries. There's nothing new about it. Believers working side by side in ministry don't always get along. That's true now and it was true then:

- Paul and Barnabas came to a point of disagreement over the issue of whether to include John Mark on their next missionary trip. It became so heated that their only recourse was to split up and head in different directions, Paul going one way, Barnabas the other. (Acts 15)

- James and John asked Jesus one time if he would appoint them to positions of power and prestige in the coming kingdom, placing them to his right and left when he ascended the throne. When the other disciples heard about this, Scripture says they were indignant with the two brothers. In other words, they were steamed! Ticked off! Super unhappy! Isn't that something? Even with the Lord himself leading, teaching and training them, the disciples didn't always get along. (Mark 10)

- Paul told the Thessalonians that some people in their fellowship were busybodies. He said they were idle, lazy, just hanging around complaining and adding nothing to the ministry. (2 Thessalonians 3)

- Oh, and don't forget that fascinating reference Paul makes in Philippians 4 about two women who just weren't getting along and it was affecting the whole church. *"I plead with Euodia and Syntyche to agree with each other in the Lord."* We know next-to-nothing about this but you can be sure the church in Philippi did! This relationship was souring the fellowship of the whole church and Paul pleaded with a church leader to do something about it. Knowing how it sometimes goes, I'm not sure that leader would have been successful.

Ministry can hurt, and it can hurt especially badly when someone you've labored with side-by-side turns on you, or deserts you, or lets you down. Christian unity is pretty easy when you really like each other and when you agree on just about everything. But when you don't?

It's kind of funny how two committed believers serving together for God's glory can so easily end up on opposite sides of the fence. Maybe it's like a married couple where one partner is a snorer. He (or she) isn't even aware of it and just sleeps the night away, snoring strong. His spouse is more than aware of it because she can't get to sleep, but when she tells him in the morning how he kept her awake, his answer is, "It wasn't me. I never snore."

Maybe a starting point for Christians serving in ministry together doing better, is to do away with the preconceptions and false idealism that imagines a kind of honeymoon relationship forever and ever. Yes, it can be really good, but it will take more than just expecting it to be good.

Two thoughts to end this with:

1. Be biblically realistic about ministry and the people who serve. We are still sinners and there will always be problems in Christian relationships.

2. Don't be one of those people yourself!

ONE MORE THING

You know the old saying, "When the going gets tough, the tough get going." You don't need to tell anyone else but do a little self-evaluation on how you've done when ministering together with someone else and it's all gone downhill.

06

I USED TO BE SHY

My first "girlfriend" was a cute red-headed girl in 6th grade. I don't remember how we ever got to be a couple, because as a rule I was scared of girls back then (okay, I actually still am!). But somehow we each ended up wearing a baby bracelet with the other's name on it. We danced together at the 6th grade parties that some of the parents held in their homes. We were a celebrity couple!

Coincidentally, we actually shared the same birthday, March 15. That year in 6th grade, when the Ides of March came around, our teacher announced to the class that it was our birthday and had the class sing to us.

You know what I did? I lifted up the lid to my desk and stuck my head as deep down into it as I could! You might say that I was just a little shy back then.

I still am.

And that's not always been an easy thing in ministry. Studies show that as many as 40% of the population are introverts. Although the terms "shy" and "introverted" are often used interchangeably, they are really not quite the same. I should more accurately refer to myself as introverted, which, by the way, is not a bad thing at all … except maybe to extroverts who sometimes seem to have a hard time understanding us.

From an article by Kendra Cherry[1], here is a good summary of some of the main components of introversion:

- Being around lots of people drains your energy.

- You enjoy solitude.

- You have a small group of close friends.

- People often describe you as quiet and may find it difficult to get to know you.

- Too much stimulation leaves you feeling distracted and unfocused.

- You are very self-aware.

- You like to learn by watching.

- You are drawn to jobs that involve independence.

I look at a list like that and go, *yep, that's me.* I said that's been a problem in ministry, but I need to explain. It's not a problem to be introverted. That's the way God made a whole lot of people and we introverts are a much-needed counterweight to you extroverts out there.

I've been on plenty of church boards over the years and I've seen this mix in action. Extroverts tend to be

---

[1] Kendra Cherry, 8 Signs You're an Introvert (Understanding Introversion vs. Extroversion), *Verywell Mind*, May 2022

quick thinkers or maybe more accurately, quick talkers. They tend to do their thinking out loud. When discussing an issue, they most often jump right in with thoughts and ideas and decisions, sometimes even contradicting themselves as they talk because they haven't thought it all through before plowing ahead.

One of my favorite co-workers was the youth pastor at one church I pastored. Matthew was and is a great friend and a trusted partner in ministry. Extroverted all the way, he could say more in five minutes than I might say in five hours. Whenever we would travel together to a meeting or conference or whatever, I could count on him carrying the conversation no matter how long the trip. And as extroverts tend to do, he would sometimes say something even when he really didn't know what he was saying.

As we were driving on a springtime trip through central Nebraska, I pointed to a huge flock of birds in some fields across the way and asked him if those were the Sandhill cranes that were so well-known in that area. He said they sure were and went on to expound on their migration patterns and other interesting tidbits. Only later did I find out they were just some regular old ducks.

Introverts, on the other hand, tend to want to listen for a while and consider things in their minds before expressing their thoughts. That may leave others with the impression that they don't have much to say, not much to add to the discussion. Actually, nothing could be farther from the truth. But since many introverts may lack confidence in themselves and be hesitant to speak up, they may end up left behind as others take the lead.

I've always loved an expression I heard way back when: "You'll never lead a cavalry charge if you think you look funny sitting on a horse."

In college, as I began to grow in my faith and in my desire to serve Christ, my biggest roadblock was my lack of self-confidence. I looked at the leaders --- both students and full-time staff --- of the college ministry I was involved with, and I felt that there was no way I could ever be like them. They seemed so confident, so sure of themselves, so at ease in leading others, so outgoing …. and then I looked at myself. No way could I ever be like that.

And fifty years later, I still feel like that!

This might not be as arresting as some other areas of pain and hurt in serving Christ, but with that backdrop, let's tackle two things that bring some "ouch" to it: comparing yourself to others and being misunderstood or not appreciated for who you are.

COMPARISONS THAT COME UP SHORT

I wonder if Simon felt inferior to Simon. Here's what I mean. You know who Simon Peter is, more commonly known as Peter. He was the de facto leader of the twelve men that Jesus chose as his apostles. Without a doubt he was the most vocal! Let's add it up.

Taking just the Book of Matthew to represent the four gospels, Peter is quoted some eleven times, speaking about 135 words. That might not sound like much but it is far and away more than any of the other disciples. Then you add his ten speaking appearances in the Book of Acts that totaled several thousand words. And don't forget that he ended up writing two books of the New

Testament as well. All in all, Peter was the spokesman, the leader, the best known, the CEO, the lead pastor kind of guy among the twelve.

Then there's the other Simon, sometimes known as Simon the Zealot. Let's count up the times he was quoted in the Gospels. Let's see, in Matthew, it's, uh, zero. In Mark, hmm, still a zero. Luke? Nothing. Surely in John, but no, he still hasn't said a word. A quick read-through of Acts comes up empty. And if you're looking for any books he wrote in the rest of the New Testament, you can look from Romans through Revelation and you won't find him there either.

In other words, Simon was there but hardly anyone noticed. That doesn't make him a loser, not at all. Are you kidding? Jesus chose him to be part of perhaps the most select group ever assembled! When the God of creation chose to come to this earth as a man and to select twelve men to be his closest associates, Simon was one of them. Imagine that on your resume! Simon was anything but a loser.

And yet how easy it would have been for him to feel like one, at least compared to the other Simon. His was a background role among the twelve but what a role to play, walking with Jesus the Messiah for three years, being front row to the unfolding of the eternal salvation story. Wow!

As you have served in some kind of ministry role, have you ever felt that comparison pressure? That you don't measure up compared to someone else? That you're not good enough because you're not like the others that you believe have it so all together?

I sure have. From my first year in ministry to my fiftieth, I've played that losing game of comparing myself to others in ministry around me:

- I've already told you how hesitant I was to get into ministry in the first place because I didn't feel I measured up to the others around me.

- In nine years on Cru staff, I never felt good enough.

- Some of the worst times I had through all my years as a pastor were when I attended pastor conferences. I'd look at the other men who all seemed so confident, so motivated, so together, and invariably I'd think, *What in the world am I doing? I don't belong here. I don't have what it takes and I don't have what these men do.* And even though I knew that wasn't exactly true, I still let it dominate how I thought. More times than not, I'd leave those conferences feeling worse than when I arrived.

- And even in these last few years of ministry, as much as I've enjoyed working with military families, that same old sense of failure, of not measuring up, of not being as good as the others around me, has dogged me.

Now I know I don't need to be that way. I know that God called me into these ministries and that he considered me qualified. I'm just telling you that even knowing that, I still would compare myself to others and come up short. I've got a feeling that many of you do the same thing.

In another book, I described what someone has called "the phantom." It's the idea of constructing an image in your mind of what the perfect person would be in your setting …. the phantom. So, for example, if you are a pastor, you envision what the perfect pastor would be, the phantom pastor. This person would:

.... love people so much

.... love the Lord even more

.... lead people to Christ left and right

.... build all those people up as disciples

.... give the best sermons, a mix of exquisite Bible exposition and fun, but with serious and totally practical application

.... love everybody in the congregation no matter how they treated you or how unresponsive they were to your unbelievable teaching

.... well, you get the picture

Whatever ministry role you have, you can never measure up to this self-created phantom. I never have. It's a recipe guaranteed to produce guilt, dissatisfaction, regret, and if left unchecked, eventually it produces resignation. One way or another, whether you actually step out of the role or stay in it battling the phantom, you lose your confidence and you lose your joy. I'm convinced the enemy has this towards the top of his list of how to defeat the believer who starts out wanting to serve the Lord and make a difference in lives.

WHEN YOU'RE NOT ACCEPTED FOR WHO YOU ARE

I can't speak so much to what extroverts face in not being accepted by others, but I certainly can for us introverts. And you introverts should appreciate this because you probably don't want to speak up for yourselves!

When you don't say much, people often think you don't have anything to say. For any extroverted ministry leaders who are reading this right now, the last thing introverts want is for you to say something like, "Will, I can see that you haven't said anything yet, so how about you tell us what you're thinking?" No, chances are the person is thinking things through and if she or he has something they think is worthwhile to say, they will.

Early on in my ministry, at one of those conferences I loved so much, I had a strange thing happen. A conference leader came up to me during a break and asked me what was wrong. *What was wrong? There wasn't anything wrong.* But because I was quiet and hadn't spoken up all that much, he assumed that I was unhappy, discouraged, depressed …. something had to be wrong! No, I was just being me.

Someone has expressed it like this: "I have an introvert hangover. I'm totally exhausted from too much human interaction."

Or as another introvert has quipped, "I'm a social vegan. I avoid meet."

The first rule of an introvert club: there is no club.

Thank goodness!

And one more. The people who always complain that I don't speak enough never seem to actually listen when I do speak.

In one sense, an introvert is handicapped when it comes to ministry because good ministry demands involvement with people. But it's just as true to say that extroverts are handicapped when it comes to ministry because good ministry demands deep and meaningful interaction with people.

So really, when you come down to it, whatever your personality makeup is, it's good and it's bad so far as being in ministry. And there's nothing wrong with that. In fact, God takes real pleasure in seeing the Body of Christ function well with its very differing components. 1 Corinthians 12 is in the New Testament for good reason. Here's a sampling of some of what it says:

> *Now the body is not made up of one part but of many. If a foot should say, "Because I am not a hand, I do not belong to the body, it would not for that reason cease to be part of the body. And if the ear should say, "Because I am not an eye, I do not belong to the body," it would not for that reason cease to be part of the body. If the whole body were an eye, where would the sense of hearing be? If the whole body were an ear, where would the sense of smell be? But in fact God has arranged the parts of the body,* **every one of them, just as he wanted them to be.** *If they were all one part, where would the body be? As it is, there are many parts, but one body. (emphasis added)*

What a delightful way to put it. God loves extroverts and God loves introverts and everyone in between. And he uses extroverts and introverts and everyone in between because they are all needed to fulfill the Body of Christ and to accomplish God's work. Extroverts may thrive in meeting and connecting with as many people as possible. Introverts may find their sweet spot in going deeper with a few.

You might excel in upfront ministry, giving talks and teaching and leading worship and sharing the gospel with everyone you meet. You might excel in behind-the-scenes ministry, leading a small group, praying, doing administration, setting up tables and chairs. Whatever. God made you the way you are, so stop apologizing for it. Just go do what he's called you to do.

By the way, Simon the Zealot wasn't the only quiet apostle. Peter's brother Andrew rarely said a word through the gospels. Maybe that was because his brother talked so much that Andrew never had a chance! But when Jesus was about to perform the miracle of feeding the thousands with just a few fishes and loaves, who was the disciple that knew where to find that food? It was Andrew. He was the one who had met a young boy and knew that he had a little lunch with him. Sometimes it's the extrovert who makes a real difference. Sometimes it's the introvert. How about that?

Bottom line, after all these years, I can say I'm an introvert and proud of it!

ONE MORE THING

- Whatever you are, extrovert or introvert or a mix of the two, are you good with it? Are you comfortable in your own skin?

- What do you enjoy the most in ministry, upfront or behind the scenes? How are you maximizing the way God has shaped you?

- Forget for a minute how others might not accept you for who you are. How are you doing in accepting others for who they are?

07

THE PREGNANCY

Well, this was a new wrinkle. She was pregnant and I had to figure out what to do about it.

Now, wait a minute, no, this wasn't about me. Let me explain.

I was directing a campus ministry at a large state university, and I had a full-time staff team of five. One of them was a great, fun-loving guy we'll call Ryan.

Ryan had a different style, a different personality, a different approach to things, more so than just about anyone else I have ever worked with in ministry. He brought a unique flavor to our staff, and it was a good flavor, one that added something to our team.

I enjoyed working with Ryan that year and he did a good job in his ministry. He loved the guys he discipled and all in all, things were going pretty well.

Towards the end of the school year, we were talking over this and that when he floored me by telling me that his girlfriend was pregnant. By him. And he wanted my advice on what to do.

Well, frankly, I didn't know what to say. Oh, I knew he needed to figure out whether to marry her or whether to help her through the pregnancy and together give the baby up for adoption or something like that, but as the director of the campus ministry, I didn't know what to say. This was a new one for me. I knew this was wrong, I knew he had sinned, I knew it couldn't be ignored, and I knew that I ought to know just what to do about it. I just didn't know what that was.

I've been in many, many similar situations since then and I still don't have a sure-fire, works-every-time answer to handling something like that. I've seen it mishandled many a time --- and other times handled well, and yet even then producing more grief than was there to begin with.

In one church I pastored, the former pastor had been arrested on shoplifting charges. The church board decided to dismiss him as pastor. When I was hired, I came into a church sharply divided over how that had been handled. One side felt the board had been much too lenient with him and thought he should have been tarred and feathered and hung out to dry. The other side felt the board had been excessively harsh. They believed the pastor they loved and learned from should have been forgiven and allowed to continue his ministry. So where do you go with that?

I know one thing; sometimes you can't win for losing, no matter how well you handle these kinds of situations. And count on it, if you're serving the Lord, sooner or later you're bound to face things like this.

Sometimes you've just got to laugh and call it a day. A friend who pastors a church tells of a woman who had been especially helpful in a church fellowship event, organizing the food preparation, handling the serving, just taking care of the whole thing. But a few months later, some other church members approached the pastor to complain about the verbal abuse they had received from that woman. Okay, now what would you do at this point? Think it over a minute, get the appropriate Scripture in mind and decide how you would handle it.

Here's what the pastor did. He pulled together all those involved to talk it over. The woman walked out of that meeting in a huff. He tried again in a second meeting, this time privately with the woman and her husband. It went worse. As the pastor suggested she needed to do something to better manage her anger, she broke out crying, fell on the floor and curled up in a ball. Soon after, they left the church.

Have you been in any Matthew 18 confrontations? Jesus laid out a process there in dealing with the sinful behavior of believers:

- When someone has sinned against you, go to him, just the two of you, to show him his fault.

- If that doesn't succeed, then take one or two others (who have some connection to him and to the situation) to try again.

- If that fails to gain a good response, then tell it to the church.

- And finally, if he refuses to listen even then, treat him as you would a pagan or a tax collector.

I've heard that passage of Scripture taught, expounded upon, exposited, examined, illustrated, encouraged and urged ... many, many times over the years. I've taught it myself.

I have rarely seen it work.

Now wait a minute, don't get a rope ready to string me up for heresy. And please, whatever you do, don't start a Matthew 18 process to deal with my sin.

Jesus knew exactly what he was saying. He said it perfectly. He laid out how believers should deal with persistent sin in the body. Everything in that passage is correct and stands as the model and standard of what to do.

Did you notice, though, that Jesus also recognized the stubborn reality of human nature and sin? If step one doesn't succeed (and it often will not) then go to step two. If step two doesn't work (and it often will not), go to step three. And if step three doesn't work (and it often will not), call it a day.

Inevitably, if you are involved in ministry, full-time, volunteer or whatever, you will be involved in this. The reality is, it will not always end well.

In one of my first ministry roles in a church, I was appointed to deal with a woman who had a way of irritating those around her with her habit of doing things her way and only her way, no matter what church leadership wanted her to do. Turns out that no one else wanted to confront her so they turned the job over to the new guy.

I tried. I failed. She got angry. She stayed angry with me for thirty years and made a point of making my life miserable whenever she could.

Ah, nothing like sweet Christian fellowship is there?

Here's an especially sad one. A friend tells of a Christian band he sang in for a number of years. It was great --- good music, great friendship among the members and positive and fruitful ministry for the Lord. It was one of those situations you just love to be a part of.

And then it wasn't. One of the band members, married with children, announced that he was leaving his spouse and moving in with another partner in a same-sex relationship. As you can imagine, this just blew up the band. They talked with the member, church leadership got involved with counsel, encouragement and challenge, but to no avail. They did it all right, but the person was determined to move in that direction. In fact, the band member involved later commented, "I've had much trauma healing from my previous marriage and from my church. I will never excuse their behavior."

So am I saying never to confront wrong behavior? Not at all. Jesus says, when needed we should, at the right time and in the right way. What I am saying is to be prepared that it may not go well. You parents know that. Your child disobeys and misbehaves; you step in to correct him; you do a good job --- and your child says, "Thank you, Mom. I really appreciate that advice and I will change what I have been doing and be forever grateful for your loving help."

Yeah, right! It doesn't often go like that, but that doesn't mean you shouldn't do what you should as a parent.

So, too, in ministry, you will face times of having to deal with a believer, often a partner in ministry with you, who needs correction. Just be ready for the reality that it may not go well.

But we'd better turn things around here for a minute. Writing this --- and you reading this --- it may sound like **we** are always the good guys having to put up with and deal with those other believers who need to straighten up and fly right!

Not so. We are all sinners, we all stumble and we all need correction occasionally. Do we ever make life miserable for those believers who try to lovingly correct us?

I like what a friend of mine says about her experience as a church leader over a number of years. She tells of having to confront two people who had bruised others while heading up an outreach event. One person responded well, the other didn't, but then my friend commented, "Probably the biggest lesson for me during those years was learning how to confront others. I am hoping that I confront much better now and in a timely manner, that I didn't just learn how to confront and then leave it there."

When I was a rookie staff member with Cru, at the end of my first year, my director sat me down for a year-end evaluation. It didn't go well. Actually, it was terrible. I had shared an apartment that year with another rookie staff guy, who had struggled somewhat in his first year in the ministry. My director felt that a good share of the blame for that fell to me. He said that I had really let my roomie down, that I hadn't been done a good job helping him and so on and so on with a number of other things.

Guess how I reacted to this confrontation? Mad, upset, unhappy, argumentative, disagreeing, put upon, unfairly treated … well, you get the idea. I certainly didn't respond, "Thank you, Bart. I really appreciate your observations. I know that you have my best interests at heart and that your insights will help me to become a better person. Thank you. Is there anything else you'd like to add?"

Now I did respond better as time went on and as I considered the things he had said to me, but my initial response was anything but positive.

Sometimes, I think we in ministry focus our attention too much on how to confront someone else and what their response is and not enough on being confronted and what our response is.

This gate in Christian service swings both ways.

ONE MORE THING

What's been your experience in confronting and being confronted? Anything you plan to change the next time around?

08

EVERYTHING HAPPENS FOR A REASON (AND OTHER UNHELPFUL CHRISTIAN CLICHES)

Singer-songwriter John Mayer said, "Someday, everything will make perfect sense. So, for now, laugh at the confusion, smile through the tears, be strong and keep reminding yourself that everything happens for a reason."

And noted theologian Marilyn Monroe (for you younger ones, she was actually a famous actress back in the 1950s and 1960s) remarked, "I believe that everything happens for a reason. People change so that you can learn to let go, things go wrong so that you appreciate them when they're right, you believe lies so you eventually learn to trust no one but yourself, and sometimes good things fall apart so better things can fall together."

We could go on almost forever with quotes from well-known people telling us that everything happens for a reason. Actress Drew Barrymore said, "I believe that everything happens for a reason, but I think it's important to seek out that reason; that's how we learn."

Let's suppose that all of these people are right, that everything does happen for a reason. And let's concede that Drew Barrymore has it right when she says we need to figure out what that reason is. Here's the problem: that thinking is not really biblical.

I know that many of you have already jumped to Romans 8:28. That's a good place to head: *And we know that in all things God works for the good of those of who love him, who have been called according to his purpose.*

Now is that the same thing as saying that everything happens for a reason? Well, not quite. The verse states that:

….. **in all things** (that does cover everything in our lives)

….. **God works** (not some indefinable force in the universe but the God who made us and loves us and sent his Son to die for us)

….. **for the good** (not necessarily what is most pleasant, enjoyable or welcomed at the time and, most importantly, not the good as we define it but as God does)

….. **of those who love him** (this verse applies to believers, not the world at large)

….. **who have been called according to his purpose** (well, that opens the door to a huge question: just what is the purpose of God in the lives of those who love him?) (emphasis added)

83

A fuller exposition of what this verse means in the overall context of Romans 8 would take us far past the goals of this book, and honestly, far past my abilities as a Bible teacher.

So let's make a couple observations. There is an important difference between the suggestion that everything happens for a reason and the truth here that God works through everything that happens.

The verse is not saying that God **makes** bad things happen just so people will learn life lessons that will help them. No, bad things will happen, period. They happen because we live in a broken world. They happen because every last person on this earth has a sin nature. Bad things are part of this life because there is an enemy of God and of everything and everyone connected with God.

BAD THINGS DO NOT TURN INTO GOOD THINGS

Nor is it saying that God magically turns bad things into good things. Bad things are still bad things. If your six-year- old is diagnosed with cancer, with no hope of making it to age seven, that is a bad thing. If a husband cheats on his wife and abandons her, that is a bad thing. Now, Romans 8:28 is saying that God can work in and through any and all things, including the worst of them, for the good of those who love him, but that is not the same as saying that everything happens for a reason, as though God initiated the bad things. Let's not try to squeeze God into our superficial thinking.

Someone has used the phrase "coffee mug Christianity" to describe how we can so easily use cliches to try to make sense of life and to try to get through the hard times of life.

Here are some examples you've probably heard:

- "It is what it is."

- "God never gives you more than you can handle."

- "God wants us to be happy."

- "When God closes a door he opens a window."

- "Let go and let God." "God wants you to be healthy and wealthy."

- "I'll be praying for you."

There's nothing wrong with good sayings so long as they accurately reflect Scripture. But there is something wrong with them if they fall short of that goal.

My overriding purpose in this book to is consider how we can keep going in walking with Christ and serving him, even through all the challenges, obstacles and pain that so often accompany ministry. Anything short of that is like taking an aspirin for a broken heart. It's not going to get the job done.

Picture this with me. Turn to Hebrews 11, often called the hall of fame of faith, and read through the great faith exploits listed there. Let's see, we've got Abel commended for his faith (even though he was murdered by his brother Cain); Enoch was taken straight to heaven without dying (that sounds appealing to me); Noah did a great job believing God in the most challenging of circumstances, and then there's Abraham, who gets several notices for his great faith.

On it goes with Isaac, Jacob, Joseph, Moses' parents (I love that they get a mention), Moses himself and many more. Fantastic stories of God at work through the faith of his people. Now the writer of Hebrews knew full well the backstory of all those people and their lives, and so do we if we've read the Old Testament accounts. They weren't perfect people by any means, nor was there anything easy about their lives and all they went through. Their faith was crucial to how God worked through them, but their faith didn't eliminate the really difficult things from their lives.

THE LIST TOOK A TURN FOR THE WORSE

The writer wasn't finished with his list though. In the last section of the chapter he adds these people to his group of believers with great faith:

..… others were tortured and refused to be released

..… some faced jeers and flogging

.…. others were chained and put in prison

.…. they were stoned

..… they were sawed in two

.…. they were put to death by the sword

.…. they went about in sheepskins and goatskins

.…. they were destitute, persecuted and mistreated

.…. they wandered in deserts and mountains, and in caves and holes in the ground

Hmm, that doesn't seem to square with saying that God wants us to be happy and healthy and wealthy. I don't think it jives with the idea that when God closes a door he opens a window. And it definitely does not mesh with the mantra that everything happens for a reason and we just need to find what that reason is. I've seen people twist themselves into knots trying to come up with a reason why God allowed (or caused?) something bad to happen in their lives.

Nice-sounding cliches can take us only so far. If that's all we've got when we run into the tough times of ministry, chances are we're not going to make it. If we think God owes us nothing but good things because we are serving him, it's unlikely we'll hang in there when it seems the good things are absent and the bad things are overwhelming.

Try this variation on the tired old cliché that people say so often: "Just remember, everything happens for a reason. We just have to pick ourselves up and look on the bright side of life."

Once I spent the better part of a day waiting with a young couple for their baby to die. It was their first child and they were so excited. But the news was bad immediately after delivery. There was too much wrong and nothing to be done except hold her and love her and wait for her last breath.

"Pick yourself up and look for the bright side?" Really?

There's an oft-used expression in sports about playing with pain. Chances are about 100% that if you regularly do anything athletic for any length of time, sooner or later you'll have an injury. It might be very minor or it might be major but it will likely be painful. You then have a choice: quit playing or play with pain.

I don't want to overstate this, but if you are serving the Lord, there is a 100% chance that sooner or later you will have pain in your service. You then have a choice: quit or keep going, even with the pain.

Hebrews 11 says that those Old Testament heroes of the faith kept on going.

Hebrews 12:1-3 says we should, too. *"Therefore, since we are surrounded by such a great cloud of witnesses, let us throw off everything that hinders and the sin that so easily entangles, and let us run with perseverance the race marked out for us.* **Let us fix our eyes on Jesus**, *the author and perfecter of our faith, who for the joy set before him endured the cross, scorning its shame, and sat down at the right hand of the throne of God. Consider him who endured such opposition from sinful men, so that you will not grow weary and lose heart."* (emphasis added)

It won't be cliches that help you do that.

ONE MORE THING

If it's not cliches that keep you going when it's painful serving the Lord, what do you find in the passage above that will keep you going?

09

THIS WON'T HURT AT ALL!

I didn't think I wanted to write this chapter. This one hurt. I'd rather have not remembered it, let alone write about it.

When I was six or seven, back in dental prehistoric times, my dentist apparently knew nothing of Novocain or nitrous oxide or anything like that. I remember having several cavities drilled and filled --- and I definitely remember the agony without the ecstasy of numbed oblivion. I don't think I visited a dentist again until I was 45.

Well, that's pretty much how I remember this ministry experience.

During the time I was the lead pastor at one church, our denomination offered a church evaluation program that a prominent leader in the denomination had developed.

I liked what I heard about it. The program seemed to have a good approach to looking at a church and it promised an objective analysis that would identify strengths and weaknesses, accompanied by a prescription for steps to take to strengthen and build the church's ministry. Our church was doing okay but not great, and it seemed to me that this could be helpful in moving us forward as a church.

I did have several minor misgivings about it. For one thing, I'd seen plenty of these kinds of evaluations accomplish little more than adding a large summary notebook that would end up on the pastor's shelf, little used and little accomplished, but at least they always looked impressive.

For another thing, the program stated the church in its entirety must enact their prescription of a list of steps to take following their evaluation, no exceptions, no leeway, or the evaluation would be withdrawn. That seemed just a little extreme to me in negating the local leadership of a church and defaulting it over to an outside entity. I was a little uneasy about that part.

Overall, though, I welcomed the idea and thought it could be a healthy step for us to take as a church. Despite the somewhat pricey cost, we bought in and started the process.

The major elements included a lengthy written survey for as many of the congregation as possible to complete. An extended weekend visit of the denominational leader, along with several other pastors or ministry leaders he had chosen to be part of the team, would follow. The weekend would conclude with a congregational meeting to summarize the results and to outline the prescription plan for the church. Assuming the church accepted the plan, there would then be an additional visit or two by the president's team to ensure good follow-through on the plan.

THE WEEKEND BEGAN

So we got started, promoting the survey over a period of several weeks before engaging the congregation to complete it. There was a good response in terms of the majority of our people filling it out. As I filled out my own survey, I noticed that the questions trended a little more toward the negative than I would have expected. It just seemed to open the door to anonymous criticism. Not that that would ever happen in a church, right?

By the way, do you have those people in your church or group? I mean the kind who just seem to love to criticize? The ones who know better than anyone else? The ones who have an axe to grind? I had a sneaking suspicion this survey might just draw them out like Monday morning quarterbacks after their team lost the big game on Sunday. That's human nature even redeemed human nature.

Anyway, that door opened wider during the evaluation team's weekend visit. They scheduled a number of meetings with various groups in the church: leaders, Sunday School teachers, various fellowship groups, etc. I thought that was a good idea and would provide a wide range of perspectives. What I didn't realize was that the open forum those meetings provided would also provide another platform for the ones who just wanted to complain.

Now don't get me wrong. Not that I enjoy it, but constructive criticism is a healthy thing. We all need that. I sure do. I already knew many of the weaknesses of our ministry, including my own as a pastor, but I also knew that I was likely blind to many others.

Will Sanborn

If there is an opposite to constructive criticism, I think it would probably be called griping. Oh my, did this open the door to that!

As an example, several years earlier our leadership team had made a ministry decision that not everyone agreed with. Maybe I should emphasize that just a little more strongly: **NOT EVERYONE AGREED WITH IT!**

Christmas was on a Sunday that year and we weren't sure how we wanted to handle that. We always held a Christmas Eve service that was well-attended and that drew in many from outside the church. We (meaning our leadership team of the elders and staff) debated how best to schedule the services. We were an average-size small church with just a single Sunday service. We hat we ended up deciding that we would hold the Christmas Eve service as usual and make that the worship service for the weekend. We would not hold a service on Christmas morning that Sunday; instead, we would encourage people to celebrate Christmas at home as a family or to feel free to attend another church that morning.

Did I mention that not everyone in our church agreed with that plan? Not everyone on our leadership team agreed with that plan. You may not either, and you or they may well be right. But that's not the point.

The point is that those who disagreed --- including one or two on the leadership team --- couldn't let it go. Their unhappiness with that decision had percolated for several years and had bubbled over at times. And now, what a perfect opportunity to vent their frustration through this survey and the open forums and the entire weekend.

Ouch!

Now there's nothing unusual about disagreements in a church. Or in a workplace. Or in a home. The only place where there's never disagreement is where someone lives alone. Even then he or she probably argues with themselves.

Maybe you've seen the cartoon where a guy is finally rescued after spending years by himself stranded on a deserted island. As he described to his rescuers how he had survived and showed them the simple hut he had built for himself, they asked him about the two other structures on the island. The guy pointed to one and said, "That's my church." Then they asked what the other building was. "Oh," he explained, "that's where I used to go to church but I didn't like the music there."

The thing that disappointed me in how the evaluation team handled this was that they took most everything at face value, whether it was a valid criticism or not. That reopened old and lingering wounds in the church with no effort to address and heal those wounds. That is a prescription for disunity.

IT WAS ALL DOWNHILL FROM THERE

It got worse …. at least for me. The team came in on a Thursday and on the schedule was a Friday night dinner with my wife and me at our home. On paper, that had sounded like a good way to start things off. Little old Pollyanna me!

They had a surprise in store for us. After a period of small talk, my wife and I shared with them the painful account of how one of our sons was battling cancer with the prognosis still in doubt. As any of you who are

93

parents would understand, that was far and away the biggest thing on our minds that weekend.

Until, that is, the team lowered the boom with their statement that they felt I should resign as pastor of that church.

Right then.

At the dinner table.

Before the evaluation weekend even began.

They believed I had taken the church as far as I could and that it was time for new leadership. Now, in our fellowship of churches they didn't have the authority to decide that or to make that decision for our church, but it was what they felt should happen.

My wife and I were floored. This came out of the blue, like an unexpected tornado. I had no inkling they were thinking this way.

I told them I couldn't and wouldn't make a decision like that, not without time to think and pray and to talk with our leadership team to get their perspective. To save you some time if you're wondering what the outcome was, I ended up pastoring that church for several more years, several good and positive years.

Are you ready, though, for the most painful part of this whole episode, even more painful than what I just described? I asked that evening, and then again at other times through the weekend, why hadn't they let me know before that night, at least a hint of what they were thinking? Why not allow me to be prepared to discuss such a momentous suggestion?

Several weeks later, I asked that of the denominational leader in particular, as he was in charge of the process. He assured me they had not talked about it or made any decisions before coming to town that day. He stated that it was only after some discussion right before coming to our house that they had decided to say what they did.

Fast forward several years. I was at a regional meeting of pastors that included one of the men who had been on that evaluation team. As we chatted, and unprompted by me, he brought up that weekend and confessed that, yes, they had indeed discussed their plans before that night. He said they had already decided earlier that week to tell me I should resign. Sadly, he told me the denominational leader had lied to me.

I had suspected that, but to hear it straight out like that was a terribly painful body blow. To have a key leader in your denomination do that is hard to understand and even harder to accept. Apparently, though, this wasn't an isolated incident. Eventually, the denominational board asked him to step down from his position.

I look back on that weekend with mixed feelings. I think there were some good results from it. It pushed us as a church to sharpen our vision and to look hard at what we could do better in our ministry. It motivated me personally to do the same. And as some in the church rehashed old grievances, it showed our leadership team that we needed to leave those things behind and to focus on the things we should and could do to be what God wanted us to be in our community.

There was no question, though, this one really hurt. It left me wounded and wondering, *why in the world would*

I want to keep being a pastor? I questioned if I was good enough. I questioned if the church wanted me as their pastor anymore. I felt like a failure. When ministry hurts like that, it's not easy to keep going.

MINISTRY DOES HURT

I know I'm not the only one, not by a long shot. I think the reason you're reading this book is because you have experienced the pain of ministry. I know, too, that many of you have gone through much more painful and difficult things than I have.

I have a good friend who has pastored for a number of years. He is a gifted and faithful man, an excellent teacher of the Word. At one point in his ministry, though, he fell into a depression, the kind you just can't shake or talk yourself out of. As you would hope, most people in his church were understanding, patient and encouraging.

As the weeks went by and the depression deepened, that understanding, patience and encouragement began to wear just a little thin. In fact, it moved from sympathy to judgment, from patience to irritation. Some felt it was a spiritual issue for which he was to blame. The reason was a medication imbalance that, when corrected, made all the difference, but before that, he experienced not just the misery of depression but the hurtfulness of the unfair judgment of fellow believers. How hard it is to keep on going through that.

Even harder, though, is the feeling that God himself is against you or that he has let you down. It's natural to think that if you're serving the Lord, the least he can do in general is make things go well for you. When they don't, the pain can be unbearable.

Another close friend has served long and well in a parachurch ministry, yet he has done so with a deeply wounded heart. He and his wife had one child. When that child was a high school senior, she died in a car crash driving to school one morning. No alcohol, no drugs, no storm, no other driver, just a crash that somehow happened and that took her life.

Some of you have been there. Others of us can hardly imagine the shock of hearing the news, of getting that phone call, of trying to take it in. How do you recover from something like that? How do you go on with the things of life? How do you keep serving the Lord when he has allowed something like that to happen?

His wife went on, but not her soul. She never really recovered from the loss of her only child. How could she? Many years later she went on to be with the Lord. And my friend? Well, he has kept going, still serving in a very fruitful ministry, but it's been with a hurt in his heart that will never fully heal this side of heaven.

So how come? Why doesn't God make things go well for believers who faithfully serve him? There's a story about an old Quaker who had been through a lot, and one day he got pretty honest with God in his prayer. He said, "Lord, I think I know why you don't have very many friends. It's because of the way you treat the few ones you do have."

In our own life, our son made it through his battle with cancer, although it took some years and much pain and struggle. Even now, though cancer-free, the physical and emotional toll the cancer took on him remains with him every day. In a similar way, our experience took a toll that remains with us years after the fact.

For right now though, we'll leave all these questions to the theologians and philosophers. Our focus is more on the day-to-day challenge of continuing to serve the Lord even when life makes it awfully hard to do, and sometimes, it will definitely be very hard to do.

ONE MORE THING

"I have told you these things, so that in me you may have peace. In this world you will have trouble. But take heart! I have overcome the world" (John 16:33).

I know we've thought about this verse before but try something else with it this time.

….. There are four sentences. Sorry for the grammar lesson, but which one of those four would you say is the topic sentence, the main idea?

….. It looks like trouble is a given in this world. Do you think that applies to your ministry or is it just for the rest of the world?

….. And last thing: think through his statement: "I have overcome the world." I mean, really think it through.

10

THE UNCHOSEN

I had been the associate pastor (youth pastor / Christian Ed pastor / discipleship / fill-in-the-blanks pastor!) for a few years and things were going well. The church was growing, my own personal ministry was coming along pretty well and I was enjoying what I was doing. The senior pastor and I meshed well, not always the norm in many churches.

Then he left to take another church. Interesting where things went from there.

I was appointed the interim pastor, something that intimidated me at first, but before long I began to feel pretty comfortable in the role. We brought on a young youth pastor intern, a recent Bible college graduate, whom I was responsible to train. I loved doing that.

As some months went by, I settled into the role and to my surprise, I began to feel that this was something I'd enjoy doing permanently. Now, I had never planned on being a pastor. I started college with the goal of being a meteorologist, not a pastor. In some ways I had ended up in church work almost accidentally, but here I was starting to think that I'd like doing this for real.

The church, of course, had begun the process of looking for a new senior pastor. In that kind of church that process would go like this: they would form a search committee made up of about five or six people representing various segments of the congregation. Following the lead of the church board, they would begin advertising for candidates for the position as described in the job description. As applications would come in, the search committee would then determine who were viable possibilities and then schedule interviews with several of them. Eventually they would settle on the top pick who would then be invited to spend a weekend at the church, followed by a vote by the congregation whether or not to hire that individual.

As that process moved along, I began to wonder if I should put my name in to be considered for the position. Back and forth, back and forth, I just couldn't decide whether that would be a good idea or a really dumb one. Some people from the church were urging me to apply, but I worried that if I did, then wasn't selected, it could ruin what had been a really good situation. To this day I'm still not sure what the right decision was, but I chose not to apply.

I have to admit that underneath it all, I kind of hoped the search committee would choose me anyway. Kind of silly when I look back on it. It would be like a young woman wanting to be chosen Miss America, but instead of competing in any pageants, she just sits in the audience hoping the judges will see her and award her the crown.

As the interim pastor I served on the search committee and for several months I watched the members debate about the possible candidates. No one seemed to be winning over a strong majority and things appeared deadlocked.

Then came a meeting I'll never forget. As the committee members debated again over the prospects, one of the members took the bull by the horns. He said, "Let's face it. We already have the perfect candidate right here in front of us. It's time to just make up our minds and choose him."

Well, I figured he meant me. I mean, who else could he mean? Nobody else really stood out from the crowd and it sure sounded like he was pointing the finger at me.

I was ready to humbly accept when the next thing he said blew that thought to bits. He continued, "Listen, we all know it's Robert. Let's just get this over with and schedule him to come in for a weekend and make him our new senior pastor."

Hey, wait a minute. Robert is not Will!

Before I knew it, the committee had agreed. They voted to invite Robert in, he came, the congregation approved, and he was the new pastor.

Wow, I've got to say that hurt my pride. Looking back, though, I can see how silly it really was. If I felt God was leading me towards that position, I should have said so and put my name in for consideration. And if I didn't put my name in, I should have just helped with the selection process and been ready to work with the new pastor.

You may never have been in a situation like that, but I'm willing to bet you've had similar experiences where you felt you were passed over, that you weren't recognized, that you weren't given credit for what you'd done. It's human nature to want to be recognized and valued; when you're not, it's human nature to resent it.

Resentment. Bitterness. Jealousy.

I think one of the most hurtful areas of ministry is right there, and it's all inside you. Feeling unappreciated hurts. It's a hurt that easily festers and grows. No wonder God speaks to it in Hebrews 12:14-15, *"Make every effort to live in peace with all men and to be holy; without holiness no one will see the Lord. See to it that no one misses the grace of God and that no bitter root grows up to cause trouble and defile many."*

Do you want an ugly reminder of how bad this can get? Just consider Haman. Do you remember him from the Book of Esther? He was the righthand man of King Xerxes, the powerful Persian monarch, and as the king's righthand man, Haman had plenty of power himself. You'd think that would have been enough for him, but --- and this is too often the case for so many of us --- it wasn't.

Haman was obsessed with hatred for a man named Mordecai, a Jew living in exile in Persia along with his cousin Esther, who through some amazing work by the Lord, had become the queen. The problem for Haman was that this man Mordecai just didn't respect him at all.

As a great official in the king's court, it was expected that all the citizens would bow down whenever Haman showed up. Everyone did, that is, except Mordecai. He just wouldn't do it. Scripture doesn't explain exactly why he wouldn't. It could be that as a faithful Jew, Mordecai wasn't about to bow down to anyone but the Lord. Or it could've been that there was a longstanding cultural issue involved. Or maybe Mordecai just couldn't stand the guy!

Whatever the reason, he wouldn't bow down, and that really got to Haman. He was ticked off big time. He believed he deserved respect and when he didn't get it he was determined to make Mordecai pay.

Take a break from the story and think about this. How have you responded when you felt passed over? When someone else got the credit you felt you deserved? When you got the short end of the stick one way or another? You probably didn't handle it the way we're about to see that Haman did, but just maybe that spirit of resentment and bitterness took hold in your heart and spoiled everything around you.

I'm embarrassed to recount another episode in my ministry when I felt passed over and I resented it. When I was in campus ministry, I developed a new approach for training ministry leaders. I presented it to the national leadership, and they enthusiastically accepted it and developed a plan to use it that coming summer. That felt great and I really looked forward to leading that, but when the assignments came out, they had chosen someone else to lead the program; they just included me as an assistant. Now what's your guess on how I felt about that? Let's just say I headed to that assignment with a sourpuss attitude you could have sensed a thousand miles away.

This can get to be an ugly part of ministry life. It sure did for Haman. His jealousy was so ugly and intense that it drove him to concoct a plan to rid the country, not just of Mordecai, but also of all of Mordecai's people, the Jews. He convinced King Xerxes to authorize the plan and for the moment it looked like Haman would get everything he wanted.

What he actually got was what anyone always gets when he or she lets jealousy and resentment consumes them. Unknown to Haman, the king was about to honor Mordecai for an act of his that had just come to the king's attention. The interplay that follows between the king and Haman is priceless. Even if you already know the story well, read again how this went in Esther 6:6-11:

> KING XERXES TO HAMAN: "What should be done for the man the king delights to honor?"

> HAMAN THINKING TO HIMSELF: "Who is there that the king would rather honor than me?"

> HAMAN TO THE KING: "For the man the kind delights to honor, have them bring a royal robe the king has worn and a horse the king has ridden, one with a royal crest placed on its head. Then let the robe and horse be entrusted to one of the king's most noble princes. Let them robe the man the king delights to honor, and lead him on the horse through the city streets, proclaiming before him, 'This is what is done for the man the king delights to honor!'"

> (in other words, "I want to dress up and play King!")

> KING XERXES TO HAMAN: "Go at once, get the robe and the horse and do just as you suggested for Mordecai the Jew, who sits at the king's gate. Do not neglect anything you have recommended."

Can you imagine how Haman felt when he heard those words? Do this for Mordecai the Jew? Are you kidding? I doubt Haman heard anything past the word, "Mordecai." This was the last thing, and the worst thing, that Haman could ever have imagined happening to him. His angry resentment had consumed his thoughts and now it was about to end his life.

In humiliation, Haman did as the king commanded and paraded Mordecai through the city streets as the crowds cheered --- not Haman but his enemy Mordecai. As the next chapter records, Haman's end came swiftly; the king sentenced him to hang on the very gallows that Haman had prepared for Mordecai.

"See to it that no one misses the grace of God and that no bitter root grows up to cause trouble and defile many."

I don't know if any of us will have our resentment of others grow into such a dramatic ending but be assured the principle always holds true. When we allow the resentment of being passed over, the bitterness of not being recognized, the anger at someone else receiving the credit that we felt we deserved, the results will always be the same. When we do, that becomes a hurt in ministry that could have been avoided.

ONE MORE THING

Read Luke 14:7-11 and see what you think on how that applies.

11

HOW SHALL I LEAVE THEE? LET ME COUNT THE WAYS

I grew up in the Philadelphia area and I am a die-hard Philadelphia Phillies fan, and "die hard" is just the right description. From their start in 1883, the Phillies have lost more than 11,000 games. That's the worst record of any Major League Baseball team. Since baseball teams play more games every year than any other professional sports teams, that makes the Phillies the worst of any teams anywhere, anytime. We Phillies fans wear that as a badge of honor.

Early on, I learned what it meant to have my heart broken by the Phils. In 1964, when I was 14, they were doing great all summer long, building a sizable lead in the National League, but in late September, the wheels came off. The Phillies lost 10 straight games and finished in second place. For a young teenager, it felt like the end of the world. If I had only known then how many more times the Phillies would disappoint me as the years went by!

Ministry is filled with disappointments. Great dreams, great plans, great hopes don't always (or even often) produce great results. Really, there's no surprise there. All of us in ministry are flawed people. All of the people we are working with are flawed people. We're working in a world dominated by the Prince of Darkness. To me, that all seems to be a recipe for disappointment.

Please don't misunderstand. You and I are unbelievably privileged to serve the King of Kings and to bring the incredible message of the gospel to people desperately in need of that good news. And when some people respond in faith and are reborn, there is resounding joy in heaven. Even more, when those believers continue to grow in Christ and reproduce in the lives of others, how rewarding that is to those who helped it along.

To continue that baseball analogy, although you and I have the most opportunities in the most seasons to win, we can expect a lot of losses along the way. All I mean to say here is that it doesn't always go according to plan. Your ministry may not always move forward successfully. Your team won't always win the pennant.

We don't have to look any farther than something that happened with Jesus in John 6. Early on, the chapter explodes with two amazing miracles:

….. Jesus fed 5,000+ people from a little boy's lunch bag of two small fish and five little loaves of bread.

….. Jesus walked on the waves of the Sea of Galilee as his terrified disciples looked on in fear and amazement.

The stage was set for an eruption of faith and discipleship. Thousands of people fresh off a miracle, the disciples reenergized, Jesus teaching them, there could be no holding it back now.

But just the opposite took place. As Jesus taught and interacted with the people and their religious leaders, and as he made claims about himself that they found hard to understand and accept, the most surprising thing happened.

Verse 60 says, *"On hearing it, many of his disciples said, 'This is a hard teaching. Who can accept it?'"* And shortly afterwards, John adds the comment, *"From that time many of his disciples turned back and no longer followed him."*

Are you kidding me? Who could have anticipated that? If we had been there back then, I think we would have expected a groundswell of faith and commitment that not only would have produced thousands upon thousands of new believers, but also that many others who had been casual followers would have become devoted disciples. It didn't happen.

If it didn't happen then, it's not going to always happen now. I think one of the hardest and most painful parts of ministry is when you've invested in the lives of people, then those people walk away. Sometimes they even turn on you and leave in anger.

In the early years of one church I pastored, one couple seemed all in. They were involved in leading a Bible study group and were enthusiastic about the church's future. Somewhere, somehow that all began to change. Their enthusiasm waned as their unhappiness grew. Here's an edited excerpt from their letter of resignation from the church:

I tried unsuccessfully several times to reach you this evening by phone and was unable to do so, so I have chosen a method of communication I really don't like to convey my feelings over this turn of events with you. We are taking a stand for the sufficiency of Scripture in every area. If this is the plan you have for the growth of the church, we cannot have a part in it and it's good that we learn early on that we were laboring under a misunderstanding that you and we were on common ground as regards the sufficiency of the Word of God to change lives and cause growth in the Church. We will not be involved in this kind of compromise. I may be wrong in many things I say and do but compromising God's Word is one thing I am very conscious of trying hard to avoid. I can't occupy two positions -- one of truth and one of what I see as compromise. Our position is not subject to compromise.

End of discussion.

People leave. Sometimes quietly, almost secretly, some-times noisily, angrily. That happened to Jesus and it will happen to you. It hurts, and if we take it personally, as though it's all about us, it can hurt terribly.

But I don't think it is all about us, at least not always. There can be so many factors involved in why someone you were pouring your life into decides to head another direction. Sure, it could be something you did or said or failed in, but it's just as likely that it's something else.

- It could be that they've lost interest spiritually, at least for the present.

- It could be that some other leader or some other ministry fits them better for where they are, or where they want to go.

- There may be other things going on in a person's life that cause them to pull back: maybe a family issue, something at work, demands on their time, and so on.

- It may well be that God has directed them elsewhere for his own reasons and not because of you.

I saw all of those reasons and more through my years as a pastor. One couple I counseled regarding their serious marriage issues ending up leaving the church because it was too embarrassing for them to be there with their pastor knowing all those issues. Another couple left after a tragic loss of life in their family; it was just too painful for them being reminded of it through being at church. And of all things, a woman left our church after being shot by her husband. Fortunately, it was a minor wound, but the deeper emotional wound seemed to squelch her desire for spiritual life.

It's a healthy thing for a spiritual leader to realize that he or she isn't the end-all of God's work! I know, easier said than done when someone you care about pulls away, but it's true. The Body of Christ is a lot bigger than my little corner of it.

Way back when, in my days of college ministry with Cru, I know I was more spiritually competitive than I should have been. When a student came to Cru for a while but then switched over to the Navigators, that felt like a personal loss to me. If InterVarsity was gaining ground on campus, I felt like we were losing ground. What if two of our students started going to one of the local church's college program instead of coming to Cru?! Oh no, we lost again!

You know what I'd compare that kind of thinking to? My first serious dating relationship. I'd fallen in love with this girl towards the end of high school, but I'd never worked up the nerve to do anything about it. When I finally did ask her out during my freshman year in college, it was so exciting when she said yes and we began dating. What I didn't know at the start — because she hadn't told me — was that she was already in a steady relationship with another guy. That began the better part of a year of a competitive relationship to see who would win. Well, the other guy did and she and I broke up, although, technically I broke up with her, or at least that's what I tell myself now.

Here's what I mean. If I had really loved her then, my real interest would have been her happiness. If the other guy was the best one for her, then I should have welcomed that because I was seeking her best. Obviously, I didn't handle it like that because it was way too much all about me.

Isn't that all too often how we handle ministry? We get competitive and it's all too much about our success and self-satisfaction. I don't mean to say it doesn't hurt when someone leaves, especially when they do it in a negative and hurtful way, but God's Kingdom is a lot bigger than my little corner kingdom.

Still, losing someone you've helped spiritually is a disappointment that eats away at your sense of worth and your sense of success. Here's one more anecdote from a pastor friend, this one just a little unique and probably like nothing you've ever dealt with, but the principle is the same regardless.

Two businessmen, both prominent members of his congregation, ran afoul of each other. One man ran a counterterrorism (CT for short) organization training people in this specialty. The other owned substantial property out in the country. They decided to join forces where the landowner would build a CT facility on his property. They developed the plans and moved ahead with construction. The CT guy even moved his family out to the property.

So far so good …. until the CT guy was found to have had major financial issues which he hadn't disclosed. Things went south and a huge battle ensued. The pastor brought them in for a meeting but that didn't go well. The landowner accused the CT man of fraud; the CT guy jumped up and started screaming at the landowner. Despite the pastor's best efforts, the CT guy stormed out of the meeting; soon after, he and his family stormed out of the church, never to return.

I love the pastor's comment afterwards: "Had these kinds of things been my common experience, I would have bowed out of the ministry long ago."

My hope is that you don't bow out either.

ONE MORE THING

Review Jesus' parable of the Sower in Luke 8. It seems that out of four potential believers, only one really continued on. The other three fell away for one reason or another.

So how's the percentage been in your ministry?

12

THROW THE FLAG, REF!

It was just a regular old committee meeting at my church, the kind I had sat through hundreds of times, talking about this or that, this plan, that report, this issue, that problem.

But something was a little different at this meeting. One of the members seemed just a little edgy. Well, maybe more than just a little. He seemed upset, almost angry, and the longer the meeting wore on, the more it seemed to me that his anger was directed towards me. I'm not always the most perceptive guy, but even I couldn't miss this.

So out in the parking lot after the meeting, I asked him about it. I thought maybe something had gone wrong at work, maybe he wasn't feeling well, or whatever. Uh, nope. It turned out he was unhappy about me. Me? The nice friendly pastor? And it turned out that what I had picked up during the meeting was just the tip of the iceberg. During the hour long after-meeting in the parking lot, he laid out a long list of my offenses.

There's no need to detail all he had to say; it was bad enough then, I don't want to relive it now! Some of his feelings, as I thought about them later, had merit and I could see how I hadn't handled some things well, especially in relating to him. I felt some of it was unfair and unwarranted, but in any case, I did my best to try to calm the situation and we headed to our corners, I mean, to our homes.

A week or two later I asked him to get together for lunch in hopes that we could talk it all through some more and then leave it behind for good. Wasn't going to happen. In some ways, his feelings had grown even stronger and more deeply entrenched. This is where it got all the more interesting.

THE REF DIDN'T SEE IT

You know how it goes in football sometimes when a player is penalized for unsportsmanlike conduct? Maybe he threw a punch at another player? More often than not, it seems, it turns out that he was just responding to something the other player had done to him, but the ref didn't see that first move, he just saw the response. So who gets flagged? Not the guy who started it all, but the guy who got caught responding.

That's how it went with this, or at least that's how it seemed to me. After talking with him several times, and then with his wife as well, they both felt that I hadn't responded the way I should have to his criticisms. They saw him being the aggrieved and me being the aggriever!

Now honestly, I would have to say that I could have done better. Had I had a do-over, I think I could have responded to his criticisms in a much more helpful way, but I ended up feeling just like the player who got flagged for the personal foul. My response wasn't as good as it could have been, but hey, he had clobbered me while I had just given a little shove back.

Have you ever felt that way as you've served the Lord? Have you felt that you were treated unfairly? That others acted worse than you, but somehow you ended up getting the penalty?

This happens in ministry all the time (in life in general, not just in ministry). You probably know the story of Joseph from Genesis 37. He was #11 in a family that included 12 brothers. His father Jacob's favorite, Joseph, was doing just fine into his teenage years until he made too much out of a dream he had and bragged about it to his brothers. That didn't sit well with them and before long, poor old Joseph had been sold off to a band of desert nomads, who in turn took him to Egypt and peddled him off there. That led to slavery and to prison and to the rest of his life away from home. That's a lot of grief for next-to-nothing wrong on his part.

That's the way it goes sometimes. Somebody else does the wrong and you get the grief. As the youngest of five brothers myself, I've been there and done that. When my oldest brother would come home on leave from the Navy, he was the family disciplinarian. Now, when something bad happens with a bunch of brothers you know that no one is going to own up to it. So my sailor brother's method of determining guilt was to have us each hold five pound lead weights in both hands with arms straight out; the first one to drop his arms was obviously the guilty party. Gee, I wonder who lost that test every time?

In the New Testament, as the Roman soldiers marched Jesus towards his crucifixion, they called out a man in the crowd to come and carry Jesus' cross the rest of the way. Simon the Cyrene was his name and I can imagine him thinking, "Hey, wait a minute! You're the guys doing this horrendously unfair execution. You're the bad guys. Why am I being picked on to do the dirty work for you?"

THE FLAG'S BEEN THROWN ON YOU, NOW WHAT?

So what do you do when you feel that something like that is happening to you? You're going along, doing a good job in your ministry, and suddenly the flag is thrown and you're the one penalized! That's a hard question and it's one I haven't always successfully answered. I know the basics:

- When criticized, your first move should be to consider it honestly to see if it's true. Now I didn't and don't like doing that, but I always knew I should.

- If it is true, then do something to change it!

- If it's not true, or maybe just partially true, there's no point in arguing back. More often than not, that just makes things worse.

- And there's not a whole lot to gain in arguing with the ref for throwing the flag on you. Chances are one in a thousand that the ref will change his mind.

- Scripture says of Jesus, *"When they hurled their insults at him, he did not retaliate; when he suffered, he made no threats. Instead, he entrusted himself to him who judges justly."* (1 Peter 2:23) And that reminds me that I'm not Jesus! Neither are you.

- Which brings me and you to a simple prayer: "Lord, forgive me for my response and help me to be more like you."

Even then, though, these things don't always have a happy ending. That episode began a slow (but accelerating) movement toward him and his wife (who was also a leader in our church) leaving the church. They didn't verbalize it so much as just gradually faded out of the picture.

His wife's closing words added to the pain of the whole episode. She blamed me for failing him. She said she knew her husband was immature and was prone to outbursts like that, but I should have built into his life better and maybe he wouldn't have had to blow up at me like he did.

Well, in theory I couldn't disagree with that. Had I done a better job in leading and building him, maybe it never would have gone down that road. I still felt unfairly attacked, but in all honesty, I know I don't receive half the criticism I really deserve --- so a little undeserved criticism is probably good for my soul!

Back to Joseph and all he went through, the heavy price he paid for others' issues and actions. When it was all said and done, some forty years later, Joseph said it better than a storywriter could have imagined. He told his brothers: "You meant it for evil, but God meant it for good."

Ouch. Ministry hurts. It's not always fair. Life isn't always fair. Sometimes we bring the pain on ourselves, but sometimes it comes for no good reason and for nothing that you've done. Either way, it hurts. But either way, God is still there.

ONE MORE THING

Think of a time when you felt you were unfairly criticized for something. How did you respond? If you had it to do over again, would you do it any differently? And if you are unhappy with how you responded back then, is there anything now you could do to make up for it?

13

LET'S HAVE SOME FUN

I f you have to do some crying as you serve the Lord, you might as well do some laughing along the way, too. Isn't there a Bible verse somewhere that says something like, "They went out crying and came back laughing?"[1]

A long-time, veteran minister recounts several episodes she's experienced over the years:

- Teaching teen-agers always brings some interesting discussions. The lesson was "Jesus knows us and has experienced everything we could or would ever go through." As I was emphasizing the point, and possibly repeating

---

[1] I know that those of you who are perfectionists have already located that verse in Psalm 126:6 and the correct wording of "Those who sow in tears will reap with songs of joy." And you are shaking your heads saying he is misusing that verse, that it has nothing to do with all this. And you are right, but hey, you can relax a little because this chapter is all about having a few good laughs along the way because you sure need them if you are involved in ministry!

myself and taking too long doing it, a voice from the back piped up, "Except old age!"

- As superintendent of the third through fifth grade Sunday School department, I was preparing for the opening lesson. A student came in early and spent his time walking up and down the rows of chairs. He finally chose an unlikely one in a fairly strange place. When I asked him why that chair, the student, the son of the high school football coach, explained, "Because it says Green Bay!"

- Coming down the church hallway with my coffee, I was pondering whether I should continue teaching Vacation Bible School anymore. The schedule was easy enough and teaming with long-time and new friends was fun, not to mention the relaxing coffee and cookies time. But at 80 years old, it was taking an increasing toll on me each year. Just then, two boys came out of the second and third grade room, literally tearing down the hall as fast as they could. To stop them I put out my arm, assuming they would at least slow down. Never missing a step, they both high-fived me and raced on down the hall. My deciding moment: I am too old for this!

- Working with three-year-olds can be a challenge of not only knowing the lesson but holding their attention and keeping them on task. During one class, one little guy who'd just had a birthday and was proudly wearing his new digital watch to class, kept us aware of the time. So along with the lesson we also heard, "It is now 9:45. It is now

9:46. It is now 9:47." And I was thinking, "Hooray for 10:00 and the end of class!"

- I was helping in a MOPS program, working with the four-year-olds group. I had a ten-year-old boy assisting me. Of course, he was too old for the group, but he was home-schooled and had come along with his mom, who was a MOPS leader. And he was a good helper, very quiet but willing to do what was needed. The story this day was about Noah and the day when the ark was closed, the rain began, and the ark started to float. For the activity I filled large aluminum foil roaster pans with water and the children sailed their little paper boats in them. A lot of scrap paper was used up, a lot of water was spilled everywhere, but the children loved it. When we were all done and cleaned up, my ten-year-old helper said, "That was our most successful activity all weeks!" And that was the best teaching evaluation I ever received!

There are lots of good lines about the differences between men and women, and if you've been in ministry a while, you already know the differences yourself. Here's one fun one, though. Men say that women should come with instructions, but then what's the point of that? Have you ever seen a man actually ready the instructions?

And here's one I can add as a pastor. I was at a pastors' conference one time, only men at this one, and we were having lunch. We were seated at large round tables, maybe eight or ten men to a table. The several weeks before this conference, I had started having some kind of swallowing difficulty. Luckily, it only lasted for a few weeks, but wouldn't you know, it flared up at this lunch. I began gagging somewhat, and quickly headed off to the nearest restroom to deal with it. I must have been gone a good twenty minutes or more before I felt well enough to go back to the lunch. Now while women often go to the restroom in pairs or groups, men, not so much. And where women would, at the least, notice that someone from their group had disappeared for almost half an hour, men? Well, they said nothing, just went on eating and whatever. I got to thinking, good thing I didn't die back there! Knowing how men fail to observe things, I might have ended up in that restroom until the Rapture!

I have a good friend whose dad was career Air Force, so she grew up an Air Force brat. Now, that's a badge of honor for military kids, but apparently not everyone knows it. When she came on staff with Cru, and was talking with her supervisor, she mentioned being a military brat. Her unaware supervisor compassionately said, "You really shouldn't be so down on yourself like that and have such a negative self-image."

Ministry can wear on you as evidenced by a cartoon picturing a pastor changing the message on the sign outside the building to: SERMON THIS WEEK: JUST COME AND FIND OUT, MEATHEAD!! The caption below pictured two men walking by and one says, "You can always tell when Pastor needs a vacation."

A Sunday School teacher tells this one: One summer I was teaching a Bible lesson to a group of young boys. I figured the story of David and Goliath might catch their interest so I told them how God had prepared David for that day through his time as a shepherd having to defend the sheep from wolves and bears and all. I tried to describe how his slingshot worked and how David must have spent hours practicing slinging rocks at bushes, trees, rabbits and whatever, before being ready to take on something like a bear. It all seemed to go pretty well, and I ended by telling them the skills they learned now may well prepare them for how God might use them in the future. Then we went outside with stuffed animals and practiced throwing bean bags at them from a distance of five feet, then ten, then twenty. Some of them were pretty good at it. So, if you ever see a policeman nail a criminal at thirty feet with a bean bag, he might just be one of my students from that class!

Some cynic has said, "Most new pastors think they are going to change the world. Then they almost get fired for changing the order of service."

Another wise guy commented on the oft-cited statistic that in most organizations, including churches and Christian ministries, 20% of the people do 80% of the work. He suggested that the real goal is to somehow get those 20% to do more of the work!

One of my favorite cartoons defines being a small church by picturing a pastor taking a phone call at his desk. The caller is asking what time the worship service is. The pastor answers, "What time can you be here?"

And another cartoon under the heading OPTIMISTS FOR TODAY showed a pastor setting up hundreds of chairs for a prayer meeting with the caption, "I hope this is enough!"

Yeah, I've had plenty of those meetings where my optimistic side was met by the realistic side and the results weren't pretty. Once our church scheduled an outreach event for the community where we brought in an immensely popular college football coach to speak. This was in Nebraska where Huskers football is a religion that's taken seriously! No way this wasn't going to draw a huge crowd and we prepared accordingly.

We did it as an outdoor event with music and fun and games for the kids, along with food for everybody. We grilled a ton of hot dogs and hamburgers. Well, you can guess where this is going. The coach showed up, people from our church showed up (although not all of them!) and some people from the community showed up. The emphasis there would be on "some" as opposed to "many" and especially as opposed to, "Wow, what a crowd!"

Let's just say we had enough hot dogs and hamburgers left over to feed the high school down the street for the next week or two. Or three.

In ministry you are sometimes called on to make hugely important decisions. It sometimes falls to you to determine the direction, or the outcome and you had better be ready to discern from the Lord what the right call is. One of those times came to me a few years into my time at my last church.

At this church we had developed a tradition of a flag football game each fall between the old guys (that is, me and anybody from out of college to in retirement) against the kids (anyone in high school or college). As quarterback for the old guys, I took it pretty seriously and for the first few years we won handily.

Then the competition stiffened. That fall, the kids had put together a really good team that included several quality college players. I wasn't quite as confident as before. Plus, there was one guy coming to our church, a young teacher at the high school, who was also an assistant football coach at the school. The kids team wanted him to play with them, considering him young enough to qualify. I wasn't sure what to do, that is, until I watched him during the warmups.

Clark was a stud. It was easy to see this guy would be the best player on the field. What a hard decision. Should he go to the old guys team even though he was young enough to be my son? Or should he play with the kids, even though that could jeopardize our winning streak?

I prayed long and hard (for about 7½ seconds) before I sensed the Lord's leading that he should play with the old folks!

Like I said, a ministry leader often faces monumental decisions that fall squarely on his or her shoulders. I took this challenge head on, checked in with the Lord and made the call. Probably the best decision I ever made as a pastor! Clark turned out to be the best player I ever threw TDs to and we didn't lose a game for the next ten years. May the Lord's will be done.

Getting my feet wet in ministry, still a college student, I joined a number of other students for a Spring Break trip to Fort Lauderdale. The purpose was to share Christ with other students on the beach and it was quite the week. This was my first experience of sharing the gospel with anyone else and it gave me a taste of ministry that eventually led me into vocational service.

It also gave me a taste of realizing ministry might not always come with first-class accommodations. The place where we stayed was not some ritzy hotel on Fort Lauderdale's beaches. No, it was a casket warehouse. That's right. A number of us guys ended up spending the week on the second floor of this business. Caskets down below, the guys up above, and I think the caskets would probably have been more comfortable than the makeshift cots we had upstairs.

And maybe I hadn't slept well the Sunday morning I did this in church. We were observing communion (the first Sunday of the month, of course, because I'm pretty sure that's got to be somewhere in Scripture), and things went a little off script. For some reason I started the process with the juice. Now everyone knows it's bread first, juice second, but the trays of juice were what I passed to the men who were serving. I got a couple surprised looks from the elders but on we went. Somewhere between the juice and the bread, it hit me that I had done things out of order, but it was too late to change things. Besides, I'm not sure the Bible says anything about a do-over for this. After the service, a couple of the elders, assuming their distinguished pastor knew exactly what he was doing, asked me what the significance was of serving the juice first. Uh, well …

And what about when someone you work with gets mad at you, calls you some unholy names in a meeting, and storms out, leaving you shaken and anticipating the apology bound to follow the next day? One cartoon pictures a pastor sitting at his desk, cobwebs having spread all over his computer, phone, chair and himself … and the caption reads, "Reverend Schneider patiently waits for the board chairman to call and apologize."

I still can't believe this one happened, and I sure wish it hadn't. I was officiating a wedding along with another pastor at his church --- the bride from my church, the groom from his. There was a room just off the front of the sanctuary where the two pastors and the groom waited for the processional to start.

Things were going just fine until …. until they weren't. First, I think I needed to make a final bathroom stop. Then the groom did. And of course, then so did the other pastor. I can't remember the exact order, but I think this nervous trio made at least one more round.

Unknown to us, the wedding coordinator in the back of the church had started the processional. I don't know what she was thinking --- other than assuming the men up front weren't doing a merry-go-round back and forth to the men's room. You've probably guessed by now, that yes, the bride and her father had started down the aisle.

Now, one of the best parts of a wedding has to be the groom watching his chosen walk down the aisle to stand beside him and the bride walking towards him in anticipation. Well, not this one. We did eventually all get out there and we did eventually seal the deal --- and the couple is still married today some twenty years later --- so what do you think, no harm no foul?!

There is no way you serve in ministry of any kind for any period of time without embarrassing yourself. For me, I could spend the rest of the book recounting those times. Here's one more. We were in the middle of a worship service; the music team was leading a song up on stage while I sat in the first row thinking about what I would be doing next.

I obviously wasn't thinking very well, because as they finished a verse of the song, I strolled up on stage, thinking they had finished the entire song. They stared at me, like, "What in the world is he doing up here?" while

I calculated what would be the best way to minimize the embarrassment and get off the stage. A little laugh and a sheepish grin was the best I could come up with on the spur of the moment, and down I strolled, knowing full well I'd be the butt of some good jokes after the service.

Things happen. Like the cartoon picturing a pastor greeting a woman at the door after the service. She looks at him and says with some surprise, "You're asking where my husband is this morning? Right where you buried him last week."

Financial guru Warren Buffett once said that the secret to his happy marriage was his wife's low expectations. Maybe that's the secret to a successful ministry, find some people with low expectations!

Some things are funny only after a lot of time has passed. There was one person in my church who, without fail, would let me know how good her former church was. Ah yes, what an encourager she was as she told me about her former pastor and how wonderful he was. It lifted my spirit seeing her every Sunday, but at least she was exercising her spiritual gift…The gift of discouragement.

It's good to be able to laugh at yourself. And you might as well because other people already are!

ONE MORE THING

When's the last time you had a good laugh? If it's been a while, watch a fun show, find a funny book, call a friend who knows how to cheer you up. Do something, but don't let the pressure, worry, or pain of ministry eat you up.

14

SOLDIER ON

I started my ministry working with college students. I've ended by working with middle school students. If I go much longer, I'll probably end up in the church nursery working with one-year-olds! Which reminds me of a fun cartoon I saw once. An older lady sits in a rocking chair holding an infant. She's thinking to herself, "Bea asked me if I could fill in for her in the church nursery just for today for a few minutes while she used the rest room. Let's see, that was thirty-four years ago ...."

Actually, one of the great privileges of all my years in ministry has been my final full-time work. For several years I've been involved with Club Beyond, Young Life's military branch, working with military teens at the Army's Fort Carson in Colorado Springs. Middle-schoolers at my old age. Who would have thought it? One of the benefits I've found in this ministry is that it seems that many people at Carson look at someone like me on post, an older man with short hair, and assume that I must be a retired officer. I've never been addressed with a respectful "Sir" so many times in my whole life!

When I looked into this ministry and eventually applied for the position, I honestly thought they would tell me, "Thanks but no thanks." After all, I did not have a military background, I had never had any involvement with this particular organization, plus I was old enough to be these kids' grandfathers. In truth, I was old enough to be a grandfather even to some of the young staff I worked alongside!

But they said yes, so let me tell you why I've considered this such a privilege. I've always appreciated our military and their sacrifices for all of us and our nation. I had never, however, really given much thought to the sacrifices that military families make.

When I was looking into joining this ministry a friend told me something that really caught my attention. He said that he had grown up a Navy brat and that whenever someone found out that his dad was in the Navy, they would ask him to tell his dad thank you for his service. Well, that's great to do and it's something I have regularly done myself many times.

He went on to tell me, though, that never --- not ever, not once --- did anyone ever tell him, "And thank you and your mom for your service." Wow, that really caught me. I had never thought of it that way, that spouses and children of active-duty military are serving as well, because of the sacrifices that they must make. For example:

- For the middle school kids (children of an active-duty soldier) that I have been working with, by

131

the time they are in 8th grade, they have already moved an average of seven or eight times as their mom or dad is transferred to another post. I've had some students that have moved eleven or twelve times! Imagine what it's like to have to leave friends and schools and everything else and constantly have to start all over again. There are some benefits to that, of course, but all in all, that's awfully tough.

- That's true for the spouse as well, of course — packing and moving and starting all over … only to have to do it all again and again and too soon.

- Then there are the deployments, sometimes long, often repeated. For months at a time, the mom or dad is gone, and the family is left behind.

- Often those deployments have been too dangerous places. Since 2001 to the time of this writing, the United States has been at war. Let that sink in. For any military brat under twenty, they've known nothing, but a nation engaged in conflict. Imagine the fear of wondering if your dad or mom will come home at all, or if he or she will make it home but be wounded in body or mind or spirit or all three.

When they do come home safe and sound, it can be a joyous occasion. While doing this Club Beyond ministry, I would occasionally substitute at the schools on post. One time I was teaching a third-grade class when I noticed some people gathering in the hall outside the door. At first, I wasn't sure what was going on, but then a soldier in full uniform walked into the classroom along with the principal. He stood there silently at the front, waiting until his daughter, Bella, finally noticed him. She screamed in joy, ran to the front and leaped into his arms. What a privilege to see this reunion as he had just returned from a deployment. The principal was standing next to me and she told me that no matter how many times she had seen that kind of scene she couldn't help but cry. Neither could I.

Our military families pay a price to serve our nation, but they soldier on.

What a great description of Christian ministry. In fact, Paul used that very picture in this passage: *"Suffer hardship with me as a good **soldier** of Christ Jesus. No **soldier** in active service entangles himself in the affairs of everyday life, so that he may please the one who enlisted him as a **soldier**"* (2 Timothy 2:3-4; emphasis added).

It's not easy to be an active-duty soldier. It's not easy to be an active-duty servant of Christ. My years in ministry have proven that to me. I've got a feeling many of you could tell stories of your own experiences that would bring the rest of us to tears.

A friend I've known since college served the Lord in full-time ministry for decades, including as the executive pastor in a large church. Read his account of what happened to end that ministry:

> *One day I walked into the lead pastor's office and found him troubled and emotionally unprepared to preach on Sunday. Together with the staff member in charge of caring for the pastoral team, we encouraged him to take some time away from work to regroup emotionally and spiritually. Several weeks went by, then a month, and nothing changed. The congregation*

began to sense that something was up and, as is often the case, began to talk and take sides as to what the issues were and what should be done about it.

Meanwhile the church elders became involved and eventually reached a consensus that the pastor was unable to continue leading the church. They worked on developing a fair exit strategy that would honor him for the positive years he had served the congregation and that would provide him with the help he needed.

However, things went downhill in a hurry. The pastor's wife, understandably, was very defensive of her husband and disagreed strongly with our decision that he needed to step down. She proceeded to make her case to many in the congregation. The church split down the middle with many eventually blaming me and the elders for causing the problem. It culminated in a group of very unhappy men confronting the elders and me with what they felt were all the mistakes and sins we had committed in this situation.

As the church devolved into anger, division and ugliness, I decided that I needed to leave. It had become the most painful time in all my ministry years. My wife felt like she lost all her friends. I left the church feeling battered and bruised for doing, in looking back, what still seems to me to have been a reasonable, well-intentioned and properly conducted responsibility of spiritual leadership.

Christian fellowship can be wonderful when everyone likes one another and when everyone agrees on how things are done. When they don't, Christian fellowship can become, well, hellish.

A woman who served as the women's ministry director in her church for a number of years tells about one of those times. The church had done a huge outreach event for many years, one that was consistently successful, but a problem had developed. The women running it had become somewhat in-grown, exclusive, critical and mean. The ministry director reluctantly decided that she needed to confront the two primary leaders of that group. It didn't go well. Although one of the women accepted the rebuke, not so the other. She responded in anger and retaliation, ending both a good friendship and what had been a really good ministry of the church.

Have you been there? Have you been in a friendship, a group fellowship, a ministry team and partnership that was going great until… until it wasn't?

Another veteran leader describes one of those times. He had worked alongside a woman in their organization developing resources for evangelism. That woman had come up with some very effective and fruitful tools that greatly helped move the work forward. The two of them were friends, partners, co-laborers. Until they weren't.

She had other ideas, other values and directions she wanted to pursue, things that ran counter to the vision and goals of the organization. The veteran leader reached the point where he knew he needed to step in and stop her plans. The result? Deep wounds, conflict and a friendship- partnership ended.

Sometimes it seems like a good ministry team has an expiration date on it, you know, like a carton of milk. It's great for a while, but eventually it can sour, and when it does, it can become putrid. I don't want to overstate that, but time after time I've seen that happen. It's likely that if you've been in ministry for a while, so have you.

It's important to remember that there is an enemy. Christian ministry does not take place in a vacuum. The devil is always looking to do serious damage. As the Apostle Peter warned, *"Be self-controlled and alert. Your enemy the devil prowls around like a roaring lion, looking for someone to devour"* (1 Peter 5:8).

Let me go back to where we started this chapter. My great privilege in working in a military ministry these past few years has been to see something of what our men and women in the armed forces face. There's nothing easy about it. There's nothing comfortable about combat. There's nothing safe about it.

One indelible memory I'll take from this time is attending the funeral service of a soldier killed in combat. Held in the main chapel on post, with hundreds of officers, enlisted men and women, family and friends there to honor him, the service followed an all-too-familiar script for those who have given their lives for our country.

Towards the end of the service a brief roll call was taken. A sergeant's name was called and that sergeant loudly responded, "Present." Another name was called. He, too, bellowed, "Present," his answer echoing in the otherwise silent chapel. Then the name of the fallen soldier was called, rank and last name. There was silence. It was called a second time, rank, first and last name. Again, not a sound. Finally, it was called a third time, rank, first name, middle name, last name. Silence. The impact of hearing that, and sensing the reality of his life being gone, was overwhelming. "Taps" followed.

We don't sing "Onward Christian Soldiers" very often anymore, but maybe we should. If you are serving the Lord in any capacity --- full-time vocational ministry, part-time paid ministry, regular volunteer work, occasional spiritual service of one kind or another --- you are a soldier for Christ.

Soldier on.

ONE MORE THING

Read again that passage in 2 Timothy 2:1—7 and give some thought to what Paul meant when he said, *"Endure hardship with us like a good soldier of Jesus Christ."*

15

THE FINISH LINE IS JUST THE START

You knew this was coming, didn't you? Probably every Christian in some kind of ministry has heard the story of the missionary who returned home to America after many years of faithful service overseas. There are variations of the story, but the gist of it is that while some famous person on board the ship was met by a huge crowd and received adoring attention, the old missionary? Not at all. In fact, no one was there and no one seemed to care.

Over the weeks that followed, that really got to him. He had always been committed to serving the Lord with a good heart and not for earthly rewards, but still, this was all it added up to? Bitterness slid into depression, leaving him feeling that his years of service to God had been a waste of time, a meaningless sacrifice unnoticed by people, unappreciated by God.

He confessed his hurt and disappointment to God as he questioned the Lord why all those years of service didn't deserve at least some kind of homecoming welcome and appreciation.

And in that time with the Lord, he sensed God telling him exactly what he needed to hear, "But you're not home yet."

That's exactly what we need to hear, too. And not just for what you may be thinking. It's human nature to want to be appreciated, to receive reward for good work, to feel noticed, and that others affirm that you're worth something. There's nothing in and of itself wrong with that.

But there's a lot more to it than that. Let's look at it from two sides.

THIS SIDE

There's a danger, a serious danger, in receiving accolades for your work. It tends to go to your head. It tends to make you think you're better than you are, that you're more valuable than you are, that you are indispensable to whatever ministry you are serving. It tends to cater to that insatiable need you have to feed your pride.

And that's not a good thing. I mean, would you really want to be included alongside Nebuchadnezzar on the list of people who proved the axiom that pride goes before a fall?

The first four chapters of Daniel recount a number of things about this great Babylonian king, culminating in his dramatic fall from grace. But do you realize just how great this king was? The guy was absolutely amazing:

- He reigned for more than forty years.

- During his term as king he molded Babylon into the dominant kingdom of its day, actually becoming the center of the known world.

- No nation could stand against him, including Judah, whose capital city Jerusalem fell to Nebuchadnezzar's forces in 586 BC.

- His power and wealth were staggering, literally beyond measuring.

- With his kingdom militarily secure, he focused on numerous building projects including many impressive roads and temples --- not to mention that he directed the formation of the Hanging Gardens of Babylon, known as one of the Seven Wonders of the ancient world.

- If they had the kinds of lists we're used to today, they would have read something like this:

WEALTHIEST MEN IN THE WORLD:

#1 Nebuchadnezzar

MOST POWERFUL MEN IN THE WORLD:

#1 Nebuchadnezzar

MOST POPULAR MEN IN THE WORLD:

#1 Nebuchadnezzar

SEXIEST MAN ALIVE … well, now we're going a little too far!

Anyway, Nebuchadnezzar had it all. He was on top of the world and he knew it, but when you're great and you know it, that's a recipe for personal disaster. God warned him about his pride through a dream that Daniel interpreted for him, but it was to no avail.

Nebuchadnezzar ignored God's warning through the year that followed until he hit the point of no return. As he considered the greatness of his position and his accomplishments, he thought, *"Is this not the great Babylon **I** have built as the royal residence, by **my** mighty power and for the glory of **my** majesty?"* (Daniel 4:30, emphasis added)

The point is, there's nothing wrong with success; after all, God expects us and exhorts us to use the gifts he has given us, to strive to do well, to make the most of our time and talents. Success isn't the problem. Taking all the credit for it is.

Indeed, pride does go before a fall. That's why I'm saying that not receiving accolades and credit and praise for your ministry might not be the worst thing that ever happens to you. We could make a long list of people --- the rich, the famous, the powerful --- who rose to great levels of success in their fields, only to succumb to the pride that led to their downfall:

- leaders
- politicians
- athletes
- entertainers
- business executives
- medical professionals
- Christian leaders

Will Sanborn

That's right. **Christian leaders**. They're not immune to the temptation to take themselves too seriously, to believe their press clippings, to long for and listen to the people who praise them and credit them with being super-spiritual men or women. From fame to disgrace is an all-too-frequently traveled path.

Let's be honest, we all want --- and need --- affirmation and appreciation, but it can become addictive, it can become when and where we begin to do things in ministry just for that, instead of doing them just for the Lord.

Someone has said that what is measured is what gets done. When I was in campus ministry with Cru, we had a ministry expectation of sharing Christ with at least fifteen students a week, a reasonable and good standard. You can probably guess what happened. Since we had to file a weekly report to our supervisors, it became easy to do it just for the credit. You see five students hanging out in a dorm room, you think, hey, that's one-third of what I need, let's do it! Not exactly the right motivation for sharing the gospel.

If our motivation for serving the Lord becomes the kinds of rewards that we think we deserve, something really important is being lost in the process.

Nebuchadnezzar paid a price, a huge one, seven years' worth of one, for his arrogant pride (Daniel 4:31). Maybe, had he listened more to the Lord and less to the fawning people around him, he could have avoided those years of misery and shame.

Maybe if we don't get too hung up on whether people show how much they appreciate us, we could avoid a lot of pain and disappointment ourselves.

I used to really look forward to Pastor Appreciation Sunday. Do you remember that? I think it started back in the 90s, although it has faded quite a bit from its most popular days. It was a great idea (at least, we pastors thought it was). It was an encouragement to church members to let their pastors know that they were appreciated. Sounded good to me.

But here's where it went south. The first few years with this annual tribute were great; I enjoyed the attention. But then I began to compare from year to year: was this year's gift as good as last year's? Did my church appreciate me as much as before, or were things slipping some? Should I do something more to generate a bigger gift? Once you start doing things in ministry just for the recognition and reward, you're on the Nebuchadnezzar Road.

Oh, and then my church started to forget it altogether. Let's not even talk about that!

THAT SIDE

That old missionary got it right when he sensed God assuring him that he wasn't home yet, that his real homecoming was still to come.

The Christian band Mercy Me captured that same truth with their song "Almost Home."[1]

Are you disappointed? Are you desperate for help?
You know what it's like to be tired and only a shell
of yourself.

---

[1] "Almost Home" Bart Millard, Benjamin Glover, Robby Shaffer, Nathan Cochran, Barry Graul, Michael Scheuchzer © Gaither Music Co., Ariose Music

*Well, you start to believe you don't have what it takes
cause it's all you can do just to move much less finish
the race.
But don't forget what lies ahead:*

*Almost home, Brother, it won't be long.
Soon all your burdens will be gone.
With all your strength, Sister, run wild run free.
Hold up your head, keep pressing on.
We are almost home.*

*Well this road will be hard, but we win in the end.
Simply because of Jesus in us, it's not if but when.
So take joy in the journey, even when it feels long.
Oh find strength in each step knowing heaven is
cheering you on.*

*I know that the cross has brought heaven to us,
But make no mistake there's still more to come.
When our flesh and our bone are no longer between,
Where we are right now and where we're meant to be,
When all that's been lost has been made whole again,
When these tears and this pain no longer exist.
No more walking, we're running as fast as we can
Consider this our second wind.
Almost home ….*

You already know this, don't you. And I'm pretty
sure you believe it, too, but what's off in an unseen future
is easy to forget or at least to disregard in the present.

There is eternal reward for serving Christ. There's
no shame in looking forward to that. I can still remember

many years ago hearing a pastor speak from 2 Corinthians 3 and how he pictured himself at that judgment.

He imagined himself waiting his turn in line as the Lord judged others for their service. Other believers were getting their reward, some a lot, some a little. He said he chuckled as he saw some older lady in line with just this little bitty pile of works to be judged. Maybe she had baked a pie for a church potluck or something else hardly worth noticing, he thought to himself.

Finally, it was his turn and he was pretty confident as he looked at his huge pile of Christian service --- his many years preaching the Word, the people with whom he'd shared the gospel, the churches he had built into sizable congregations, the cantankerous church members he'd had to graciously deal with, how he'd served on the local ministerial, all the money he had raised for missionaries … on and it all piled up. It was looking like Pike's Peak! He was feeling pretty good about it.

That is, until Jesus took a match to that huge pile. It began to smoke a little, then flare, and before he knew it, his enormous pile of service had become engulfed in flames and disappeared into ashes.

He said he felt the Lord look at him and say, "Well, son, your pile of works turned out to be wood, hay and straw, but still, welcome into my kingdom."

As he turned to enter, he noticed that old lady with her miniscule pile. Jesus put the fire to it, and to the amazement of that pastor and all who watched, it revealed her works to be gold, silver and precious stones. Her service that had appeared so insignificant to others was of immeasurable value to the Lord.

Just a story, but a lot of truth. Whether or not we are recognized and praised while we serve the Lord here on earth is of little importance; how much reward we gain in heaven is up to the Lord.

The promise of eternity with Jesus in heaven is what makes it all worth it. Serving Christ here on earth may be done with tears, but consider what we will leave behind as we enter eternity:

- sin
- mistakes
- unfairness
- injustice
- pain sorrow
- grief
- shame
- hatred
- disgrace
- failure
- fear
- unhappiness
- broken relationships
- embarrassment
- betrayal
- sickness

- death

In the end it will be worth it.

We're almost home.

ONE MORE THING

Thank the Lord that you're almost home and for all that will mean.

EPILOGUE

I recently saw a study with these observations:

- An average four-year-old child typically laughs about 300 times a day.

- An average forty-year-old adult takes ten weeks to laugh that many times.

I don't know who did the counting for that study, but the results resonate with what we've been considering here.

Life wears you down. The years take a toll on you physically, mentally, emotionally, relationally, and yes, spiritually. We've seen numerous New Testament passages that implore believers to keep on going, not to quit. So why all those passages? Well, it's because life does wear you down and the natural inclination is to pack it in and give up. And that's true not just in spiritual things but in so many areas of life. It might be your job, your marriage, your family relationships, your weight and health, your goals, on and on it goes. It's not easy to get to the finish line in this world because there are so many obstacles along the way.

I've been a runner for as long as I've been in ministry, not a serious try-to-win-big-races kind of runner, but a steady a-few-miles-most-every-day kind of one. And I've done enough marathons and half-marathons and 10Ks along the way to know this: it's not easy to keep going!

In many ways the longer you do it, the harder it gets. One of my brothers ribbed me a couple years ago when he said I was that kind of old guy runner who thinks he's going really fast but in reality, is barely making progress. All too true! One time I was in the last couple miles of a half marathon and hanging on for dear life. I noticed a much older guy to my right who was basically just walking. Now at least I was still running so I thought for sure I was going to beat that guy. Uh, no, every time I looked to my right, there he was, neck and neck with me.

Many years of running, with its stress, strain, aches and pains, can wear you down. Many years of ministry with its stress, strain, aches and pains, can wear you down, too.

Ecclesiastes is a fascinating Old Testament book that can feel so out of place with its seemingly dismal outlook on life. Here's a taste of it from Chapter Twelve:

Remember your Creator in the days of your youth,

before the days of trouble come

and the years approach when you will say,

"I find no pleasure in them" …

before the sun and the light and the moon and the

stars grow dark

and the clouds return after the rain;

when the keepers of the house tremble,

and the strong men stoop …

when men are afraid of heights

and of dangers in the streets;

when the almond tree blossoms

and the grasshopper drags himself along …

Well, you get the picture. If you've begun to feel like a grasshopper just dragging himself along, then you know the challenge of ministry.

It can hurt, you can get tired, and you can wonder why in the world you are doing this.

And yet, deep down inside, you still know it's worth it. Maybe you've lost a step or two along the way, but if you're reading this, it means you're still going.

So keep going.

At the end of Chapter Twelve, the Teacher in Ecclesiastes gave this summary statement: *Now all has been heard; here is the conclusion of the matter: Fear God and keep his commandments, for this is the whole duty of man.*

In other words, regardless of everything else he had to say about the ups and downs, the vanity of vanities, and what can feel like the meaninglessness of life, keep on going anyway.

Because it's worth it. In every way it's worth it. Serving Jesus Christ is an unbelievable privilege.

The best part of any race I've ever run has been the finish line. It didn't matter if I set a new personal best, if I hit the time I'd set out to run, or even if I beat that old man walking along the side of the road. What mattered was that I didn't quit. I finished the race. And that felt good.

Go finish the race God called you to run.

About Kharis Publishing

Kharis Publishing, an imprint of Kharis Media LLC, is a leading Christian and inspirational book publisher based in Aurora, Chicago metropolitan area, Illinois. Kharis' dual mission is to give voice to under-represented writers (including women and first-time authors) and equip orphans in developing countries with literacy tools. That is why, for each book sold, the publisher channels some of the proceeds into providing books and computers for orphanages in developing countries so that these kids may learn to read, dream, and grow. For a limited time, Kharis Publishing is accepting unsolicited queries for nonfiction (Christian, self-help, memoirs, business, health and wellness) from qualified leaders, professionals, pastors, and ministers. Learn more at: About Us - Kharis Publishing - Accepting Manuscript